SMOLDERING LUST

SMOLDERING LUST

THE INSIDE STORY OF A DOOMED TV SERIES

VANCE MUSE

CUTTING EDGE

The original edition of this book was published as *We Bombed In Burbank: A Joyride to Primetime*

ISBN-13: 978-1-962896-10-8

Published by
Cutting Edge Books
PO Box 8212
Calabasas, CA 91372
www.cuttingedgebooks.com

For my father

To the cast, crew, writers, and producers of Smoldering Lust: *Thank you*

PREFACE: EMBERS TO ASHES

Smoldering Lust is ashes now, fading into memory along with many other promising television series that have met the same fate — the Faye Dunaway sitcom called *It Had to Be You,* Fox's funny *Bakersfield P.D.,* the aggressively promoted *South of Sunset,* Don Rickles's turn in *Daddy Dearest,* and the well-acted *Family Album.* You may recall none of them, and don't smack your forehead trying to remember *Smoldering Lust,* either. A half-hour comedy by Jay Tarses, the Emmy-award-winning creator of *The Days and Nights of Molly Dodd, Smoldering Lust* was, it now seems, doomed from inception. NBC resented having to fool with the show in the first place and does not mourn its loss.

After green-lighting *Smoldering Lust,* the network then appeared to take a vacation from the series, pretty much ignoring its summer-long production. Four months is long time to go without notes or a thumbs-up from your boss or buyer, but Jay and company, trusted to deliver the goods, appreciated the feeling of independence — of not having to write with a numbers guy in a Hugo Boss suit looking over their shoulder.

Production wrapped in late September. All thirteen episodes were in the network's hands. But phones weren't ringing. Was *Smoldering Lust* D.O.A.?

There is so much to do to roll out a new series — marketing campaign, publicity plan — but *Smoldering Lust* didn't even have an air date. Nothing was happening because the network had yet to schedule the show. It didn't know what to do with *Smoldering Lust.* A comedy that kicked off with a corpse and treated adultery casually if not approvingly, the series was a hard sell to viewers, affiliates, and advertisers. It also looked and sounded different from its contemporaries.

Unlike a typical television comedy shot with multiple cameras in front of a live audience instructed to laugh REALLY LOUD and to obey signs that flash "Applause" with desperate frequency, *Smoldering Lust* was filmed — like a movie, with a single camera on a hushed sound stage (plus a few locations around town). Knee-slapper it was not, but *Smoldering Lust* wasn't a dark comedy, either. It was funny, but in an ineffable "Jay way" — low-key and high-style - that makes you smile more often than laugh. That went for the overall tone of *Smoldering Lust*, from its cocktail-lounge soundtrack to dialogue that whispered and purred and made you want to lean in closer.

Dusted off for its long-delayed debut, the series aired during Memorial Day weekend (when 20-to-40-somethings were doing anything but watching television). It arrived not as *Smoldering Lust* but as *Black-Tie Affair*. The network had at last turned its attention to *Smoldering Lust*, burdening the series with a flat-footed, forgettable title and burying it in a time slot known as a graveyard of also-rans and noble failures. After the third of the thirteen episodes aired, *Smoldering Lust/Black-Tie Affair* was gone, over, done. If you blinked, you missed it.

The fizzling of *Smoldering Lust* was assured by the same network executives who spent some $9 million producing the series, which was gorgeously filmed, richly scored, and starred Kate Capshaw, the blockbuster-marquee name also known for her serious chops and creds as an actor. Though Jay Tarses may never be a ratings champ, he is nonetheless a venerated craftsman in the business, viewed as an iconoclast who can deliver the creative if not the wildly commercial goods. When pressed, the money people will say that writers like Jay are worth the huge risks they take for them, and win prestige points by backing ambitious programs. In such deals Jay is represented by a small but mighty production and management firm, Brillstein-Grey.

None of these factors, though—the superior technical craft of the production, the allure of Kate Capshaw, Jay's eminence as a writer-producer, or a network's desire and initial enthusiasm for prestige programming—could save the series. Something went terribly wrong with *Smoldering Lust* sometime between the approval of the first script and the delivery of the thirteenth and final episode. The demise of the series was a humiliating defeat for its well paid producers, writers, and lead actors, and a significant financial loss for the dozens of other people who nursed the show from idea to reality—designers, drivers, musicians, electricians, caterers, carpenters.

For the better part of 1992, a core group of about forty were in the full-or part-time employ of *Smoldering Lust,* the only TV comedy ever to introduce a corpse in its premiere episode. Going into production, most of them didn't know what the show was about. Some knew Jay's previous work; a few had never heard of him. As scripts began to circulate, details of the new show got around. Morning-coffee and water-cooler talk was all about Margo and Chris Cody, an attractive, affluent couple in San Francisco whose marriage is not the happy one it so publicly seems to be.

The blond, bearded Chris, played by John Calvin, is an accidental entrepreneur, co-founder of Cody Canyon, a mail-order purveyor of wilderness gear and clothing. A pillar of San Francisco's business community, he has been married for fifteen years to Margo but has an eye on Eve Saskatchewan, Cody Canyon's star model. Slipping off to his first rendezvous with Eve (which will begin his first extramarital dalliance), he finds the body of a dead woman in a hotel-room bed. The incident, which concludes the premiere episode, gets the series off to an ominous start.

Portrayed by Kate Capshaw, Margo is a soft-spoken, leggy beauty to whom business success comes easily and enduring romance seems out of reach. The brains behind the Cody enterprise, she aches for attention in the bedroom, not the board-room, and winds up falling for the scruffy private investigator she hires to follow her husband, Dave Brodsky (Bradley Whitford). Brodsky operates his agency out of an old record shop, where he is assisted by a sharp-tongued Asian-American woman known only as Cookie (Maggie Han). When the routine case of a possibly philandering husband abruptly veers off into a who-done-it murder mystery, Brodsky panics, but Cookie keeps her cool. Both realize two things: that Brodsky is falling in love with Margo, and that Chris is innocent of the murder. By turns sheepish and cocky, Brodsky is forever bragging about how irresistible he is to women, but he can't get to home base with the one of his dreams, Margo.

The most obvious suspect in the murder case is Hal Kempner (Bruce McGill), the obsessed inventor of a gimmicky athletic shoe that he desperately wants the Codys to sell in their catalog. The militaristic Hal is forever implying that he has damaging information about the Codys.

Margo, to her surprise, finds herself growing fond of Eve, the nubile object of Chris's frustrated desire, played to perfection by the twenty-year-old Alison Elliott. Margo and Eve (yep: naming this pair Jay nods or bows to *All About Eve*) are wiser and stronger than the men in their lives, and Eve's lust for Mr. Cody, as she insists on calling Chris, is thwarted by her growing admiration for Margo. Initially coming across as a dumb brunette, Eve evolves into a near-feminist sister, a Sartre-quoting straight-A student. Her nemesis, for reasons never made clear, is Margo's officious assistant, Philip Wingate (Patrick Bristow). It is Philip who originally plants the idea that Chris is cheating in Margo's mind and persuades her to hire Brodsky.

The action unfolds on three main stages: the Cody Canyon offices in a San Francisco warehouse; the Codys' bedroom, in a wealthy, Nob Hillish neighborhood; and Brodsky's junky record shop on the wrong side of town. Key location scenes are set in a twelfth-floor suite and downstairs ballroom of a grand hotel.

Before the second episode is over, it's obvious what's meant by the peculiar title: the lust these characters feel for one another never ignites. Though most possible couplings are tried—Margo and Chris, Brodsky and Margo, Chris and Eve, Chris and Cookie, Brodsky and Cookie, Eve and Brodsky, Philip and Hal—lust is doomed to smolder away. In the Codys' world, would-be lovers look but do not touch: fool around and you could wind up dead in bed.

So what about the corpse? *Smoldering Lust* is in no hurry to solve the crime, giving far more time to leisurely exploration of the quirks and whims of its characters, all of whom are too self-obsessed to be much affected by the murder. Red herrings dart in and out of the action—Felton and Towanda, a couple who live at the hotel; a corrupt senator; Philip, who's caught shredding Cody Canyon documents by Eve (his long-lost sister, it develops). But the plot lines all return to the Codys' icy bedroom. The driving question of the series is not who done it, but who's (not) doing it with whom.

At the end of the thirteenth episode, Brodsky, who often addresses the camera directly, *Moonlighting*-style, ruminates on "the hardest mystery" to solve, which of course is not identifying the killer, but "figuring out why someone makes your heart beat faster." Whether the dead girl in Room 1216 is real or only a figment of Chris's guilty conscience is a question the show's writers will not have the opportunity to answer.

The TV audience didn't make it even this far into the six-and-a-half-hour tale. After forcing the title change to *Black-Tie Affair* shortly before its inauspicious premiere, NBC yanked the program after three episodes. We can only guess what might have happened to the characters. As for the real people who put the show together, their work goes unseen since it's unlikely the show will ever be broadcast again—thirteen episodes isn't enough to sustain a syndicated run even on an obscure cable station. *Smoldering Lust* has effectively vanished—except in these pages, which bear witness to the hopeful making and chaotic unmaking of a prime-time network television series.

CHAPTER ONE

BURBANK HO

When you call for directions to Burbank, the people answering the telephones for the people you have an appointment with are likely to make a big deal about how difficult it is to get there. "Take Highland straight up onto the Hollywood Freeway," you're told, which sounds simple enough. "But then you've immediately got to get over to the far right lane to make the first exit, Barham. You'll never make it—it's impossible." They do not suggest an alternate route, so you throw back a double dose of caffeine and head out, high with anxiety about your maiden voyage to the San Fernando Valley. North on Highland the traffic is bumper to bumper, but the newcomer can take in the sights along the way: Hollywood High, looking sleeker than a public school should on the corner of Sunset; the dragon-scale spires of Grauman's Chinese Theater (you learn to call it by its glamorous old name); the Moderne facade of the Max Factor Museum (a makeup museum!). Glance back at the giant green monster on top of the Ripley's Believe-It-or-Not "Odditorium," then, *swoop*, you're on the Hollywood Freeway.

This is supposed to be the tricky part, getting across four lanes of traffic. Flashing the right blinker, you take it one lane at a time ... the first one's easy, so's the second; then a sign: BARHAM BLVD ¾ MILE. Almost a mile? Cars are zooming to the left, right, front, and back of you, all right, but this isn't Italy's Autostrada, and it's nothing to cross the next two lanes in time to make the exit. When the traffic does get tight, other drivers are accommodating, waving you in. The ones who do threaten to cut you off all seem to be in Range Rovers, the four-wheel-drive gasoline swillers that look so ridiculous plying paved city streets (after *The Player,* who would want to be seen driving a Ranger Rover in town?). Almost leisurely, you execute the exit and think: This is what qualifies as a difficult maneuver in Burbank?

To satisfy an old curiosity, I am on my way to watch a TV show being made. I grew up on the television of the sixties, made an occasion of watching it, which in our house in Houston was just about every night. My family's set was in a style known as Chinese American, housed in a pagoda-shaped cabinet that I thought was beautiful. A somewhat stagestruck boy, I sometimes fashioned a curtain for the screen out of a Fieldcrest towel, navy and light blue, the colors alternating in a fleur-de-lis pattern. I thought the towel was beautiful, too. My parents would indulge me once in a while, taking their seats as I raised the towel on an evening's viewing: *The Ed Sullivan Show* on Sunday nights, *The Carol Burnett Show* on Mondays, *The Fugitive* on Tuesdays, *That Was the Week That Was* on Fridays, *Hollywood Palace* on Saturdays. Though I'd stopped doing this before I was a teenager—I hope I did—television remained a huge distraction from homework all through high school, years of *Laugh In* and *Batman* and *Mod Squad.* In college, overnight it seemed, I pretty much forgot about just watching TV and studied it instead, making my way through media studies and Marshall McLuhan. Television may have been a cool medium, but it was definitely not cool to watch anything then except maybe the news and reruns of *Leave It to Beaver* and *I Love Lucy.*

For more than a decade—all of the 1970s and well into the 1980s—the only show anyone I knew would admit to loving was *Saturday Night Live* and *The Mary Tyler Moore Show.* But good things were coming out of Burbank, including more solid roles for women, in TV movies, than feature films offered. Accomplished actors were making good livings appearing weekly in drama series and sitcoms. Portrayals of minorities were becoming more abundant and fairer, less stereotypical—though I wondered then and still do about the real-world effects of television on social attitudes: if it truly were a powerful medium and not just a prevalent one, surely today's vast audiences for such shows as *Roseanne, L.A. Law, Murphy Brown,* and *Melrose Place* would represent a society that is far less racist, sexist, and homophobic than our own.

A few years ago I began hearing from friends whose lives and careers had taken unexpected turns, landing them in the television business as writers, producers, designers, directors, actors. Their reports from Burbank were like nothing I'd heard before, all about the rigors of auditions and all-night rewrites, along with accounts of terrible skirmishes in the half-century-old battle between the jeans and the suits, the creative side versus the executive. I couldn't believe the number of bodies needed to put on a half-hour show week after week. Or the dollars—numbers so high, in production costs and salaries, that decimal points seemed to be missing.

I wanted to see for myself how it all happens. Living in New York, I'd caught the stage act of Julie Halston, a celebrated comic, who had been asked by CBS to develop a pilot based on her one-woman show. I thought of horning in on those development meetings, then reconsidered; I wanted Burbank, not New York. In the *Hollywood Reporter* I read about *Graham,* a sitcom revolving around a children's TV host, starring Griffin Dunne. Finally I called someone I'd known back in Texas, Nevin Dolcefino, who was now a talent agent in Los Angeles. Good timing: Nevin had just gotten word about a start-up and was angling to book clients in it. And now, coasting off the Hollywood Freeway, I'm off to watch the unfolding of that new show, *Smoldering Lust.*

Intriguing, amusing and baffling, it struck me as a the of title that could make or break a show=.

From Nevin I have the name of the supervising producer, Elaine Arata, to whom I made my pitch about hanging out with the cast and crew all summer, while they put the series together. "Cool!" she cried. "Come on out!" Before heading west I knew the show would not be typical television, either in the way it was made or in the end result. Still, it's an irresistible subject because of the pedigree of the project and because of the technical, dramatic, and writing talent beginning to assemble around the production.

Though Jay has enjoyed enormous mainstream success—he and his former writing partner, Tom Patchett, won an Emmy in 1972 for *The Carol Burnett Show,* following that with a long stint on *The Bob Newhart Show*—he has come to be regarded as one of television's maverick writer-producers (a peculiar industry conceit, since so-called mavericks in Burbank still must produce work that grabs millions of advertising-attractive Americans). A native of Baltimore, Jay met Tom in the advertising department of the Lancaster, Pennsylvania headquarters of Armstrong Cork. When they weren't writing ads they were telling jokes, eventually leaving the company to hit the road as a comedy team, Tarses and Patchett, appearing at Playboy Clubs around the country. In 1966 they ghostwrote a comedy album called "Colored Man," about a black superhero (played by James Earl Jones), and in 1971 released one under their own names. The album, recorded before a live audience, was called "Instant Replay," and consisted of sketches having to do with the observation that married men, much to their wives' dismay, have a huge appetite for watching football on television. Not maverick stuff, especially in an era of Comedy albums by such artists by such artists as Jonathan Winters, Richard Pryor, George Carlin, Lily Tomlin, and Steve Martin.

Drawing on their stand-up experiences, Jay and Tom pitched a TV series, *The Chopped Liver Brothers.* Though the pilot failed, the pair were in demand all through the seventies, landing the jobs with Carol Burnett and Bob Newhart, hitting or missing with sitcom fare for such stars as Tony Randall and Dick Van Dyke. *Mary,* Mary Tyler Moore's musical-variety follow-up to her decade as Mary Richards, was a famous miss. They had some luck with movies, writing the screenplays for *The Great Muppet Caper* and *Up the Academy,* a raunchy military-school comedy. Their 1983 collaboration for television, *Buffalo Bill,* starring Dabney Coleman as a misanthropic talk-show host, would mark the beginning of what has become Jay's signature work—quiet, quirky, rather self-conscious comedies—and the end of the Tarses-Patchett partnership. Tom would go on to create *ALF,* the hit TV series about a space alien. "We stayed together a few years too long, that's all," says Jay. "But we had a split—I couldn't write for puppets again. I prefer working with human beings."

Now in his fifties, Jay refuses to dress or act like the TV-establishment titan he is, preferring sneakers and shirt-sleeves most days, sometimes a baseball jacket, often a baseball cap. His physical presence is imposing, hulking almost, but he speaks softly, in a voice that is velvet on the ears of cast and crew members accustomed to the barking that many in his position do. He cannot stand still—if he must remain in one place he rocks back and forth on his feet—but he is even-tempered at work, sanguine and self-mocking about his success:failure ratio. "My shows never get renewed," he says, exaggerating the truth (*Molly Dodd* got snatched up for one more season by Lifetime). As the new series starts up, Jay swings both ways on its chances, sounding alternately optimistic and exasperated. "This one could really go," he says. "I mean that—a big hit." Then later the same day: "We're dead before we begin." No matter what promises a network makes to producers and writers—and NBC has made plenty to this team—nothing's a sure thing in television. "What I want to make sure of," Jay says as the production got under way, "is that we have some fun while we're working to get this show on the air. Is that too much to ask? Let's enjoy ourselves this summer." A fine sense of anything-can-happen envelops the enterprise, and I know I've found a hot spot in Burbank.

Smoldering Lust is to be filmed at Empire Studios. Sounds grand, Empire Studios, but it's anything but, tucked far away from the beautiful downtown Burbank of TV legend. As you sweep down into the Valley off the freeway, landmarks of the Media District slowly come into view through the grainy air, which is smudged with toxic wisps of gray and yellow. There's the fabulous Warner Brothers lot, the giant beige stage buildings looming against the arid mountains. Movie history was made on this lot, from *Casablanca* to *Chinatown*. Stage 4! *The Maltese Falcon* and *Mildred Pierce* were shot there. Today, *Murphy Brown* is a long-term tenant.

Empire Studios lies well beyond the old studio glamour, even beyond NBC's three-story headquarters, perhaps the blandest building in Burbank, flanked by palms and squatting a few long blocks from the Victorian gingerbread cottage built by one of the city's pioneer settlers and now administered by the local historical society. Burbank does have a history that predates its celebrated life as film and television capital. The present city, which marked its centennial in 1987, is named for David Burbank, a New England dentist who came west a decade before the Civil War and established a vast sheep ranch on land that he and his heirs eventually subdivided and sold off, land that the studios now own. The sole evidence of the nineteenth-century past is that forlorn gingerbread cottage, beyond which sprawls a vast residential neighborhood. One mile-long street of modest houses ends, across a railroad crossing, at the massive shell of a Lockheed factory, where some twelve thousand workers once assembled jet engine parts. The ailing company shut the operation down in 1990 and a lone guard watches over the abandoned plant, protecting it against vandals. Across from this sad sight lies Empire Studios.

The show is to be produced during the nerve-jangling summer of 1992, and in California, southern California particularly, it is a time of terra infirma. By the time filming begins in early June, the violent aftermath of the first Rodney King trial is a month in the past, but people are still on edge. In a desperate fiscal measure that sounds like a sitcom joke, state government employees are being paid with IOUs. Feeling out of step with viewers and markets, network executives are in a panic about competition from cable moguls and sputter about an industry-wide "pull-back," swearing they must halve production costs, sacrifice staff and projects. But terra infirma is also literal: the Landers and Big Bear earthquakes of June 28, hours apart and measuring on the Richter scale 7.4 and 6.5 respectively, send weeks of aftershocks up into the Hollywood Hills, through Beverly Hills, all the way to Santa Monica. Earthquake preparedness is big news as geologists announce that the worst isn't over: other, bigger quakes will come. Survival kits sell briskly. People are afraid to get into elevators, or to pass under freeway bridges.

Empire Studios is currently home to three budget productions, including a pair of game shows, *Bedroom Buddies* and *Infatuation*, the latter produced by Bob Eubanks of the long-ago *Newlywed Game.* The third tenant, *Smoldering Lust,* though its title may sound like another Eubanks production, is that rarity in television, a filmed half-hour comedy. Most comedies on television are videotaped with four or five cameras before an audience. This one is filmed in sound-stage secrecy, with a single camera, each scene shot multiple times to cover all perspectives, all characters' reactions. There will be no audience, no laugh track added.

It is surprising to find a major network production housed in such a modest facility, and the lack of frills will indeed cause problems over the summer. (Shooting is disrupted, for instance, whenever the game-show ruckus penetrates the studio's thin walls.) There's something appealing about the humble venue, and it's tempting to think of the proverbial gang of kids scratching up a show in a barn. Outside, the roster of parking-space assignments leaning against the dinky garage is hand-lettered.

The small lobby of Empire, painted the color of raw salmon, is crowded most mornings with game-show contestants—twenty-to thirty-year-old men in creased jeans, women of the same age sporting shaggy tumbles of hair, the kind that made Farrah Fawcett famous nearly twenty years ago. "We're a studio," the receptionist says into the telephone, speaking loudly above the chattering contestants. "We rent out to motion picture and television crews. I don't understand who you need to speak to. What do *you* do? Tell me that and maybe I can direct you to the right person."

The producers of *Smoldering Lust* are paying Empire about $15,000 a week for what is known as "four walls": space and utilities, period. Everything else must be brought in, hired out. If the show were shooting at Warner, say, or Paramount or Sony, or NBC or Fox, it would have access to personnel, services, and inventories for costumes and scenery, new construction in the studio wood shop, camera and lights, trucks and cranes. At Empire, *Smoldering Lust* must contract separately for all these essentials and also bring in its own crew.

According to the show's key grip, responsible for all scaffolding and tracks for the lights and camera, the choice of Empire is a false economy since the studio is designed for videotaped productions, not high-quality film work. "It's a cramped video warehouse," says Bill Witthans. "We need more space for the kind of lights film requires." Bill has been in the business since a sunny afternoon in 1976, when his father, a camera operator, got him a job knocking down scenery at Goldwyn Studio. Bill's first look at a vintage film stage, like an enormous hollowed-out factory, awed him. Empire's three separate stages could fit into the smallest at Goldwyn. But what's missing at Empire isn't only cubic feet. "You want thick wooden floors so you can anchor scenery by nailing or screwing it down," Bill says. "And catwalks, to secure it from above." The floors at Empire are concrete. "We have to pile sandbags around the scenery walls. And we can't do anything from above because the ceiling is too low. This isn't a stage, it's a warehouse."

A back staircase leads up to the production offices for *Smoldering Lust*. The walls are a pale mustard color, the desks and filing cabinets are metal standard issue. The harsh fluorescent lights buzz faintly. A water cooler stands next to a Bunn-o-Matic coffeemaker. Plastic horseshoes in primary colors are scattered on the synthetic no-pile carpeting. Pinned to one wall is a row of brown envelopes, where interoffice mail is collected, each envelope hand-lettered with a department name or job title and bearing an appropriate illustration: a pencil on the one marked SCRIPT SUPERVISOR, for example; *That Girl*-style bangs for HAIR & MAKEUP.

The producers' motives for filming this far from NBC headquarters aren't entirely financial. There's also the factor, or at least the powerful illusion, of independence from the network executives, who most TV writers would swear live solely to leave their messy fingerprints on scripts. Empire's wrong-side-of-the-tracks location does not encourage drop-by company. So what if the stages and storage areas are a little cramped, the soundproofing rather thin, the offices bleak? At least the suits won't be walking over after lunch. For that reason *Molly Dodd* was filmed in a warehouse in Queens, New York. Empire, out on the edge of Burbank, meets one of Jay's golden rules of TV production: Never set up shop within walking distance of a network. "Otherwise," he says, "those people will stroll over whenever they feel like it."

The production team's head count varies week to week with budget vagaries. Crew members can be laid off when the costs of an episode skyrocket, to be brought back as soon as the ink

returns to black. No one likes the on-again, off-again employment, but that's how it is for roving bands of players looking for
work around Burbank during the lean years of network television production.

CHAPTER TWO
LUCKY THIRTEEN

The first scratch of the idea was Brandon Tartikoff's. Back in 1989, toward the end of his stellar tenure as NBC's entertainment chief, the boyish-looking impresario who green-lighted such hits as *St. Elsewhere, The A Team, Cosby,* and *Cheers,* had recently broken the bad news to Jay about *The Days and Nights of Molly Dodd.* And this only two years after this pat on the back about *Buffalo Bill:* "It's the best show I've ever had to cancel." But now something else was bouncing around in Brandon's expensive brain, a ball he thought Jay might run with. Jay likes Brandon, considers him a friend, almost—says that unlike his corporate fellows, Brandon never lies. Jay's always popping off about network brass, usually in junkyard language, but Brandon didn't take such rantings personally. If Jay bucked and kicked and bit the hand that fed him, well, that's sometimes what the best runners in a stable do. Summoned to NBC headquarters in Burbank after the cancellation of *Molly Dodd,* Jay heard what Brandon had to say. Which was: "I see guys in tuxedos."

We all did then, on the style page of the *New York Times,* in *People* magazine, and on the cover of *Vanity Fair.* The stars of the decade of greed and their crimes and infidelities: Sid Bass and Mercedes Kellogg, Michael Milken, Henry Kravis and Caroline Roehm, Lynn and Oscar Wyatt, Saul and Gayfried Steinberg, the Mosbachers—remember *them*? But most visibly there were Donald Trump and his blondes—Ivana and Marla and wasn't there another one? "How about," Brandon said to Jay, "a series called *Black-Tie Affair*?" He went on: the show would be about a couple, well-off, stylish, urban, social. Married a while now, ten years or so. But he's having an affair with his dental hygienist, and she's sleeping with, with … a waiter at their favorite restaurant, which is of course *the* restaurant of the moment. But the waiter's not just a waiter, he's an informant, paid by the Securities and Exchange Commission to spy on the husband. So it's all about deceit and white-collar crime, and about well-dressed spouses cheating on one another. It's all in that double-entendre: *Black-Tie Affair.*

To Jay it sounded like fun, even relevant. "I like the idea of exploring the problems of marriage," he says. "I've always been fascinated by the institution—why it works and survives, why it doesn't. And marriage now—that's an interesting arena." But he also saw a big problem with the idea. The first thing they would have to do, he told Brandon, was figure out a way to make such basically deceitful characters likable. The question, he recalls, came down to this: "How can anyone—that is, the audience—be expected to like these people if they're sneaking around on each other all the time?"

Neither man rushed an answer. More than two years passed, time for Jay to hit yet another brick wall, with *Baltimore,* a comedy about a family of musicians, set in his hometown. The unaired pilot's chief detractor was Jamie Tarses, the network's head of comedy development, and also Jay's daughter. "Not your best work, Dad," she told him in a show of reverse nepotism. By that time Brandon Tartikoff had left the network to become head of Paramount Pictures, and Jay, without his ally and admirer, was prepared for his first meeting with the network's new entertainment chief, Warren Littlefield, to be his last. He dwarfed the slightly built, redheaded Warren, who, like his predecessor, could pass for a college boy. Warren is groomed like a grown-up executive, however, every hair blow-dried into place, his beard trimmed just so. Behind the glass doors leading into NBC's top-echelon suites, Jay made no secret of his unhappiness over his five-year deal with the network, which gave NBC first option on all of his series ideas. After *Buffalo Bill, Molly Dodd,* and *Baltimore,* he had begun to feel that he was owned by an ungrateful master or, worse, that he'd struck a terrible compromise. In any case, he wanted out. "I'm giving up too much and so are you," he said to Warren. "I don't want to be here anymore. I don't care. Let me try one more thing and if it doesn't work I'll leave. Or you can pay me off now and I'll leave."

The straight talk was refreshing; no newly installed network head wants to tangle with a temperamental writer. If Jay was eager to move on, fine—that might make one less ax to drop on a ratings clunker—but Warren was game to try with Jay. Agreeing to one last round, Jay halfheartedly pitched a couple of ideas—a series based on a minor league baseball team, another with a music-driven *Fabulous Baker Boys* spin. Neither grabbed Warren, and the discussion turned to Brandon's *Black-Tie Affair,* the idea for which, it turned out, NBC owned. (Though most of Brandon's pet projects reverted to him when he left NBC for Paramount, this one didn't.)

Jay had not forgotten about *Black-Tie Affair*—and had, in fact, begun to explore the subject for himself in a play, his first for the stage. First produced at the Williamstown Theater in Massachusetts, *Man in His Underwear,* a two-act comedy set in Baltimore, has a family man in obvious midlife crisis leaving his wife for a younger woman—the same salty waters that Brandon imagined swirling around *Black-Tie Affair.* Asked whether or not the play glances off events in his own life, Jay was coy at the time, commenting only that the work is "both very personal and not autobiographical."

And so Warren and Jay agreed: *Black-Tie Affair,* whether a hit or a miss, would retire the writer-producer's obligations to the network. They'd have to pay Jay's way, however. "I'll write you a first-draft script," he told Warren. "We'll talk maybe one time about it. Then I'll go off and do the final draft. After I deliver it, you'll have five business days to decide whether you want to go ahead with the project. If yes, then it's a thirteen-show commitment. If no, then that's it, it's over, we're history. And you pay me off." The men shook hands; the necessary paperwork would be drawn up between the network and Jay's producing partner, Bernie Brillstein of Brillstein-Grey.

Though a comedy, the show will be handled through the drama department. And the decision makes technical sense, with the show produced like other TV dramas—that is, filmed, with a single camera and no audience. But the agreement also will spare the dueling Tarseses, Jamie and Jay, the agony of having to work together again. (Privately adoring, professionally antagonistic, the father-daughter relationship has struck many as one of the more amusing in Burbank.) Agreeing with the decision, Jay says he doesn't mind being handled by the drama staff, doesn't feel passed along like a hot potato: "Seems to me they've had some good ideas and some decent shows. I like *I'll Fly Away* and *Law and Order,* and there must be some others I can almost watch." Kevin Reilly, the newly appointed vice president of the department, is thrilled to be the show's shepherd. "All writers are on a pedestal to me," he says. "What they go through facing a blank page and committing an idea to it make them so incredibly vulnerable. I know because I've tried it." Kevin is aware that he is in for a bumpy ride this time, with someone who takes glee in publicly branding network people as bores, idiots, and scumbags. "Often the most talented writers are the least collaborative," says Kevin. "But they're worth it." If Kevin sounds eager to please, he is. The trait seems to be basic to his nature. But he is also particularly anxious to prove his professionalism in this situation, which is somewhat hobbled by a strange-bedfellows twist, for as everyone in Burbank knows, he and Jamie Tarses were Once an item, and Kevin would just as soon not antagonize the man who might have been his father-in-law.

In an office he keeps in an ordinary, two-story apartment house, a block from the Studio City branch of the Los Angeles Public Library, a liquor store, two car mechanic's shops, and a dance studio, Jay returns to Brandon's scenario. Jay never liked the title *Black-Tie Affair* and scrawls a new one at the top of a fresh legal pad: *Smoldering Lust.* The "smoldering" is important: if lust only smolders but never catches fire, the characters will remain likable and the sins and situations comically interesting. "None of the affairs can be consummated," says Jay. "I've got to keep the characters just *thinking* about doing it, but not actually doing it. We can laugh at *smoldering* lust."

The first-draft script of the premier episode, titled "The Girl in 1216" and dated late February 1992, lays out a fateful night in the life of Margo and Chris Cody. The opening scene fades in to a crowded hotel ballroom, where the thirty-eight-year-old Chris, a "raw-boned, outdoorsy, reluctantly attractive man," is being honored as San Francisco's Man of the Year. By his side is Margo, thirty-six, a "great-looking blond." Surrounded by smart people in evening dress, neither "appears particularly comfortable ... for reasons which will become clear." A voiceover begins, by the character Dave Brodsky, who is in his late twenties. Wearing a bellhop suit and "looking like a young George Segal, [he is] standing on the periphery, watching the action." Brodsky introduces himself as our guide—and the private eye hired by Margo to tail her husband. "To look at 'em," says Brodsky, as the camera moves back and forth between Margo, Chris, and himself, "you'd think they were the perfect couple. But move in closer and you can see those telltale signs. Signs of yearning and restlessness ... that faraway look in his eye and maybe in her eye, too. It's all so damn bittersweet you could almost cry." On extramarital shenanigans in general, Brodsky sounds a post-AIDS warning: "Why ... be out squeezing strange fruit, especially in *this* day and age?"

The other item on Chris's agenda this evening is a tryst and, pratfalling his way to Room 1216 upstairs, he finds a young woman is waiting for him in bed. But, holy gosh, she has been bludgeoned to death. Falling back on slapstick, Jay is already trying to make the story and the characters more sympathetic; Chris does not in fact cheat on Margo, and the corpse all too vividly illustrates the wages of sin. Lurching back down the hall, Chris crashes into a room service waiter, and his locally famous face is seen by half a dozen onlookers, including Felton and Towanda, a black couple who seem to be permanent residents of the hotel. In the confusion, Chris loses his eyeglasses case, a piece of evidence that will place him at the scene of the crime.

Meanwhile, Margo is nabbed on the ballroom floor by the smarmy and somewhat scary Hal Kempner, who begins to badger her about a terrific new product he has for the Cody Canyon catalog, the Toad athletic shoe. Brodsky comes to the rescue by telling her she has a telephone call. In an alcove just off the hotel lobby, Margo and Brodsky dive for one another, kissing long and hard. Breaking free and catching her breath, Margo slaps Brodsky across the face. Then dives again. "Are you totally insane?" she cries, enthralled by the good-looking detective she's put on her husband's trail. "Thirty-five thousand people could walk in here and see us." Not the stranger to illicit passion that Margo is, Brodsky explains to her that that's precisely what makes this kind of thing so thrilling. "Kiss me again," she commands, then fires questions at him about Chris's would-be mistress: "How does…the predatory little bimbo bitch look? What was she wearing? Is she taller than I am? Is she young? How *could* the rat-bastard?" The interlude ends as madly as it began, with Margo ordering Brodsky to "shut up and do your dirty little job."

BRODSKY
Fix your make-up.

MARGO
Wipe that lipstick off your mouth.

BRODSKY

Straighten your dress.

MARGO

Kiss me. (Brodsky approaches) Don't touch me.

Making his way back to the ballroom, the shaken Chris gamely tries to pretend that an enormous room-service tray has not spilled all over his white dinner jacket. Margo, joining him on the dais, asks him about the mess, then adds to it by splashing red wine on the jacket. "Our marriage is a sham," she hisses at him. "And you're a fraud." Then, plaintively and out of the blue: "I want to have a baby." Coming early in the series, the line lets the audience know that this self-obsessed pair have no children to drag through their battles. As parents, Margo and Chris might not be so amusing. "I've already got enough risky elements for a comedy," says Jay. "This show is about people jumping in and out beds, and doing other activities they shouldn't be doing. Marital torment. So it adds a sympathetic element that Margo wants children. But I'll stop there, at her *wanting* them. They can't have kids, not while their marriage is so rocky." Besides, he adds, and this may be his most compelling argument for keeping Margo and Chris child-free: "I don't want to have to deal with kids in the scripts."

Speaking now to the guests in the ballroom, Chris makes jokes about his disheveled appearance and rambles on about "my lovely wife, Margo" when he suddenly turns ashen. Across the room, tapping her watch, is an obviously peeved young woman— Eve, it develops, the Lolita of Chris's lust. Wasn't she just upstairs, dead in bed? Thinking he's seen a ghost, Chris collapses, falling off the podium. Brodsky again narrates as the episode ends, recapping the highlights, rolecalling the gallery of characters, and meditating on life and lust. He signs off with a tantalizing, tune-in-next-week hook: If not Eve, "who's the girl in 1216?"

Such cliffhangers are as old as serials, but Kevin and Warren, upon reading the script, were wary of kicking off a new comedy series with a murder. No one had said anything about blood-shed when the show was discussed. But Jay assures them that the crime is not what it appears to be, that the mystery won't consume the series; it'll be solved soon, and won't drag out like the ultimately soporific who-killed-Laura-Palmer puzzle of *Twin Peaks.* There are other questions from the network: Why is Chris Cody so bungling? Will people like a guy who flees a murder scene? Jay admits that the character needs to seem more in control of himself, and agrees to sharpen and strengthen him over subsequent episodes. "Cody's a decent guy," he tells Kevin. "You'll see." Much will depend, Kevin is sure, on how viewers react to Margo, whether they can accept her as the moral center of the story. "If we can feel for her," he says, "then everything else will follow and be fine."

"The Girl in 1216" is vintage Tarses fare, aimed above the broad sitcom target. This one pays homage to hard-boiled detective fiction and film noir. (Margo Cody and Dave Brodsky could be funny-mirror reflections of the characters played by Barbara Stanwyck and Fred MacMurray in *Double Indemnity* or Mary Astor and Humphrey Bogart in *The Maltese Falcon).* In Dave Brodsky, Jay seems to have created a younger version of himself, a connoisseur of jazz who loses his cool over a gorgeous shiksa. And Margo Cody is indeed the ideal Tarses woman, another WASP goddess in the pantheon of Suzanne Pleshette (*The Bob Newhart Show),* Geena Davis and Joanna Cassidy in *Buffalo Bill*, Megan Gallagher on Jay's short-lived 1987 ABC series *The 'Slap' Maxwell Story*, and Blair Brown's Molly Dodd. (Though considered a "women's director" in Burbank, Jay gets mixed reviews from feminists, who have noted that his heroines range from the merely goofy to the neurotic. He bristles at the mention of one critic, Susan Faludi, the author of *Backlash,* who singles out the "morose Molly" [Dodd]—a "thirty-four-year-old divorced heroine [who] has lost not only her husband but countless jobs,

boyfriends, her neighboring female friend, and even her thera-
pist"—as an archetype of the backlash against the women's
movement, "bolstering the stereotype" of the single woman
whose defects outweigh her attributes.)

Though not all the reservations about the pilot script are
resolved, the network okays the series, ordering thirteen episodes. Just like that. It's lovely news, putting Jay high above the
fray of pilot season. Every year, from January through April,
writers and producers play roulette with the networks, scrambling to deliver new-show candidates by May for fall-schedule
consideration. Hundreds of ideas may get pitched during a particularly frenzied season, and of that number a hundred, possibly
more, are okayed for pilot production. Thirty, perhaps forty, of
those get picked up, that is, green-lighted as new series, in deals
calling for four, six, or thirteen episodes. The game is hugely
expensive for the networks, who commit dollars to pilot production as a basic research and development expense, and the odds
for success are frightening, with maybe a quarter of new shows
hitting near the top of the Nielsen charts. Jay, then, with fat bird
in hand, has good reason to be pleased this season. Nonetheless,
he finds himself in a mild state of alarm. "I'm not worried about
the script, which I know is pretty good," he says, "so I thought
they'd go ahead and buy it. But holy shit. Now I've gotta solve
the murder."

Bernie Brillstein, who has been Jay's manager since 1970 and
is now his production partner, insists on a thirteen-show mini-
mum, even in these timid times when network commitments
rarely exceed six episodes. "We hate to do six shows," Bernie
says. "Six doesn't give you a chance to break in the material,
build an audience, or try other time periods. I mean, it's all over
in six. Why spend the time and money for six shows?" For the
creative side, thirteen is terrific, granting the writers and actors
time to find their voices and characters. Thirteen also releases

an avalanche of money, in the form of the network's per-episode license fee and in the same frequency of salaries for cast, crew, and production staff. For writers and producers less known than the likes of a Jay Tarses, or a Steven Bochco (*NYPD Blue*), a Gary Goldberg (*Brooklyn Bridge*), or a Marcy Carsey and Tom Werner (*Roseanne*), development moneys are eked out: first for the idea, then the script, then the pilot, then for the first four or six shows of the series.

Because Bernie's production credits include such overflowing pots of gold as the lowbrow *Hee-Haw* and the long-running *Saturday Night Live*, he has little trouble getting NBC to go along with his demand for a baker's dozen of *Smoldering Lust*. Though the deal he has fashioned is lucrative and lovely—for producers, virtually all TV deals are lucrative and lovely—Bernie, who started out pushing the mail cart at William Morris's New York office in 1955, pines for the creamier days of the past. "When I first started doing this," he says, "there were thirty-nine shows per season. Can you imagine? The networks ordered thirty-nine episodes. With thirteen repeats, that made fifty-two weeks, a whole year of programming. It was better business then."

Stoutly built, white-haired, and bearded, Bernie can be a coddling Santa or a ball-snapping shark, depending on how he feels about who's calling. Favored clients get the indulgent, savvy elder; network suits get the chomper. Interviewers get something in between. He has been wary of discussing his business affairs ever since the death of his client John Belushi by drug overdose in 1982.

But Bernie is a showman, and showmen live to talk about their shows. In his sweet mode, recalling the comedies he has fathered, he is apt to crow, "I love bringing joy to millions." A gallery of posters hanging in the Sunset Boulevard offices of Brillstein-Grey (the management and production powerhouse Bernie founded in 1983 with Brad Grey) displays the duo's golden touch, which is also a hip one: *Ghostbusters, The Blues Brothers, Wayne's World.* The client list includes Lorne Michaels, creator of *Saturday Night Live,* and spans an arc of TV comics from Carol Burnett to Dana Carvey. Along with the new network production *Smoldering Lust,* the firm also produces Garry Shandling's series for HBO, *The Larry Sanders Show.* Another credit, Stephen Frears's *Dangerous Liaisons,* seems out of place on Bernie's résumé. "Everyone thought I was nuts," says Bernie, who produced the movie during his brief tenure as production chief of Lorimar. "This was supposed to be my folly—how was I of all people going to do a costume drama, a literary thing like that and make money on it? Well, I'd seen the play and thought Christopher Hampton had written the most beautiful words in the world. So what if the tale is set in the 1700s? I don't care if it happened in 1422—the *words* were there. I thought it was real commercial, all about sex and fucking and relationships and people playing cruel games. I saw it and thought, *Dallas* with costumes."

That may be a hopelessly TV-eyed way of looking at it, but who among those familiar with the Hampton's play from the novel by Choderlos de Laclos would argue that Bernie wasn't the man to bring the story to the screen? His reputation as a deal maker, as one of the old-guard players who helped to put the "biz" in showbiz, shouldn't overshadow his passion for performers and writers. Selling *Smoldering Lust,* Bernie is quick to shout down network objections about the material being too far out of the mainstream of "identifiable, sympathetic family life," as one detractor put it. "They cried the same thing about *M*A*S*H,* and *Cheers* too," snaps Bernie. "And what the fuck was *M*A*S*H* about if not a family—people making a family far from home. And all those folks sitting around a bar in *Cheers*—now *there's* an all-American family." Same, he insists, for the Codys of *Smoldering Lust*—not the Brady bunch next door, perhaps, dysfunctional definitely, and apparently guilty of one or two of the deadly sins. But a family nonetheless. Only the most pious could fail to see that.

He knows the network will have a hard time selling the show to advertisers and to the public—"It ain't *Home Improvement*," he says—but it may not turn out to be what he hopes it will be thought of, either: a combination of *Twin Peaks* and *Northern Exposure*. For one thing, *Smoldering Lust* is locked into a half-hour format, and it's not certain that the writers will be able to execute the show's twists and turns within the twenty-two minutes left for the program after commercials. Bernie resists precisely labeling the show, but it looks like another Tarses creation that falls somewhere between comedy and drama, and for network television, the so-called dramedy may be subtle to a fault. Bernie is always calling Jay's work "cutting edge." "Everyone was applauding Diane English for dealing with abortion on *Murphy Brown*," he says. "But Jay did it sooner, on *Molly Dodd*. A two-parter on NBC. And if you look at the scripts of those two series, you'll see that they're very similar. I screamed bloody murder about that."

Brillstein-Grey Enterprises manages Jay; Brillstein-Grey Enterprises goes into production with him on a fifty-fifty basis. "We own the show together," says Sandy Werneck, the firm's executive in charge of the *Smoldering Lust* production. "We share all costs and earnings. If we lose a dollar, Jay loses a dollar." But the chances of making out are good since Brillstein-Grey and Jay aren't required to kick in unless the show's production costs start to exceed the license fee Brillstein-Grey has negotiated with NBC.

Such fees, the money networks advance on a show's production, may or may not be sufficient to cover costs. This one, about $700,000 per half hour, is generous, especially for economic times that are proving that the entertainment industry is not, after all, depression-proof. If the operation is thrifty—or better, tight—the show can possibly be produced for that amount. The truth is that most license fees could handily cover the costs of cast and crew and the usual overhead if they didn't cover producers' fees. Bosses of course pay themselves better than they pay their employees, and Jay takes no salary cut as executive producer of what he thinks of as a shoestring operation. Secondary producers are paid handsomely, draining money from other departments—and from others' salaries. As supervising producer, Elaine Arata collects $18,000 per episode, grossing close to a quarter of a million dollars for the thirteen-show run. One way the firm hopes to keep down production costs is to exclude from the enterprise the crew members' union, the International Alliance of Theatrical Stage Employees. Though the Writers' Guild, Directors' Guild, and Screen Actors' Guild are on board, the much larger IATSE is not welcome, not when the union's wage and benefit requirements would add some $20,000 per episode to the budget. Going into the production the crew is not happy about its nonunion status, which will change—thanks to a few agitating employees—before the fourth episode is completed, and Brillstein-Grey will have to pinch and pull the budget to accommodate the new financial demands on the show. That, of course, will be accomplished not by cutting any producers' fees, but by cutting back the working hours of clerical workers, "hammer rats" (carpenters), and department assistants. "There are ways," says Sandy "of making your license fee work."

Even to a business-side veteran like Sandy, the amount of money laid out by each network in license fees is staggering, totaling some $3 million every night of the week. "And that's just for prime time," says Sandy, "not counting daytime or late night. Over seven nights, that's twenty-one million. Each network, each year, six hundred million. And that's only license fees." Added to that are millions more in development and pilot costs, plus everything else: real estate (mortgages and rentals on studio and office space), promotion and advertising, all those moneybag salaries. "What must a network spend in telephone charges?" Sandy asks, shaking his head in wonder. The rich but lean operation of Brillstein-Grey makes him feel contentedly in control.

Sandy isn't citing the figures to generate pity for the networks, since hit shows can charge advertisers up to a half-million dollars for a thirty-second spot. However, if a show fares poorly in the ratings, and so with advertisers, the license fee may easily exceed revenue as the cost of commercials tumbles and the enterprise is thrown into deficit financing. To offset that, producers rush to strike distribution deals with the likes of Columbia or Viacom; buying into a production, a distributor gambles on a show's eventual sale to overseas markets. Before deficit financing and distribution deals there was the investment tax credit, "a lovely thing," Sandy says with a sigh. "It helped a great deal because even if your license fee was low you could get a huge tax break at the end of the year and defray the costs of production. But that's history."

Smoldering Lust has hardly begun and already the arithmetic of possible winnings and losses is enough to cause headaches.

CHAPTER THREE
BEAT IT OUT

First week of March: green light! By the middle of the month the series' writing team was in place. Jay's teammates: Richard Dresser and Russ Woody. Jay caught one of Rick's plays a few years back, at New York's Ensemble Studio, an old-fashioned sex comedy called *Alone at the Beach,* and managed to sign him on as a writer and producer for *Molly Dodd.* The Manhattan malaise of that show was a natural for Rick, an acerbic New Yorker by way of New England, but it had been difficult to get him to venture out to the show's production offices and studio in Queens even to see about the job. Moving out to the West Coast would have been unthinkable to Rick had *Molly Dodd* not been such a good experience, netting him two Cable Ace award nominations and one win. He couldn't refuse the offer to work with Jay again, on a show he would help shape this time. "Basically," he says, "I caught the next plane."

Russ's past with Jay dates to a night at Hampton's, a popular pub in Burbank, when the young writer walked up to Jay and introduced himself. "I thought it might backfire," says Russ. "It was very forward of me." But the admiration was mutual. Jay was a fan of *Murphy Brown*, whose original writing team Russ was a part of. Their subsequent talks led to what Russ considers his best work up to now, the four scripts he wrote for *Slap Maxwell,* which starred Dabney Coleman in another unlovable role as a scowling-at-the-world sportswriter. A California boy, Russ grew up wanting to be Rob Petrie, the protagonist of *The Dick Van Dyke Show.* "I was a lonely kid," he says. "Depressed. My brother was ten years older, I didn't like my parents. I escaped into sitcoms. Comedy was always such a wonderful mystery to me, whereas drama seemed easy. I mean, it's easy to make people cry. But to make them laugh? That's a wonderful mystery to me."

Russ welcomed the new job as a break from the madness of multiple-camera sitcoms, such as *Murphy Brown* and Linda Lavin's *Room for Two.* Such shows are driven by frenzied round-table brainstorming that forces writers into competition with one another. "It can be like high school," says Russ, who has also done time on *Family Ties* and *Mad About You.* "You see writers jockeying for position, working so hard to be the most popular. There's this enormous pressure to come up with lines that get the biggest laughs from the studio audience. During rehearsals, your colleagues actually fake these uproarious laughs at their own jokes. Third, fourth, and fifth time around they're still belly laughing. And the really sad thing is that the stars and the producers seem to be fooled by it. Fake belly laughs get rewarded. That's how you get rich in this business."

That is guaranteed not to happen in *Smoldering Lust.* Each script would essentially be the work of one writer. To be sure, the three men will collaborate, but only on the general direction of the series, and they will give each other notes on their outlines and scripts. The goal is to shape and edit each other's work, not to wrest it away, as they drive the story forward.

Rounding out the creative team are two women, veterans of Tarses productions. Elaine Arata, who was assistant producer of *Slap Maxwell* and *Molly Dodd,* has been promoted to supervising producer of the new show. An aspiring writer, she'll supplement her administrative duties by joining in the discussions that set the general direction for the series. Penny Franks is script coordinator (a couple of decades ago she would have been called script girl). In her late twenties, with long, red hair, Penny is a latter-day hippie chick who manages to stay cool even when she's in a deadline rush to type up Jay's and Russ's handwritten drafts.

For Penny, these first few weeks on the job are the best. "I love beating it out," she says, "getting it all down on paper—the characters, the relationships, the locales, the jokes. This is when you all get together to agree how it's going to pulse and play on the page. When you beat out a script." Beat it out: make it funny, make it true, make it fit the half-hour format. Beat it out: on laptops and legal pads. Meeting in diners and cafés around Burbank, the five begin to sketch out the series, using "The Girl in 1216" as a starting point.

"Hey, gang," says Jay over one of a dozen story-session lunches, "we've got to solve this murder."

"You mean you don't already know who killed her?" asks Russ.

Jay doesn't even know whose body it is. "I just thought that'd be a wonderful way to end the first episode," he admits. "But that's why we're here."

They agree that whatever the details of the murder, it must not become the pivot of the series. "It gives us a hell of a good thrust," says Jay, "but we can't let it be the story. We have to play around it. If we just solve the crime it'll be *Murder, She Wrote*. The murder can't become more important than any other element in the story."

RICK: "Like, will Cody and Eve sleep together?"

JAY: "And will Brodsky and Margo?"

RUSS: "And will Hal get his Toads into the catalog?"

Elaine giggles.

"I agree that if we get too much into the murder, we'll have a genre on our hands and we'll be expected to neatly solve the crime." Rick is thinking out loud. "The critical thing about the murder is not who did it, but the shadow it casts on the characters' lives. And don't we want the characters to live in their confusion for a while? The murder question is all part of that confusion, along with the romantic confusion. Generally, I think this show is the kind that can let a murder mystery go unsolved for a while."

"We're not plot-oriented, then?" Russ asks.

"Right."

Elaine giggles.

All the talk thus far about not making too much of the murder is not reassuring. Jay sounds panicked: "What are we doing? We're not mystery writers, we can't solve anything. We shouldn't be here. They never should have allowed us to do this. We're going to have to call the guys at *Jake and the Fat Man*. We are uniquely unqualified to solve a murder."

"Jay, we're more optimistic than you are," says Russ. "Don't forget it's a comedy."

"I don't know that—*is* it a comedy? I don't know where we're going. I don't know if any of this is going to work. Does it go anywhere? Do we even have a show?"

"That's what we're doing here," says Rick.

"What are we doing? We're sitting and talking and having lunch all day."

The murder, they decide, might even be bogus, or staged, or explained away somehow. "We don't have to know anything for sure for a while," offers Russ. "Can't we just imply 'to be continued … '?"

The series form does lend itself to unresolved stories and elastic endings, since human lives spill over into the next week; why shouldn't TV episodes? "I like to let my stories ramble on," says Jay. "In a sitcom you have that neat beginning, middle, and end that wraps everything up in a half hour. What's the point in that?" Though he admires some sitcoms, such as *Roseanne*, he hates the format's emphasis on punch lines and over-the-top reactions from a studio audience (sweetened with a laugh track). "I trust my audiences to know when to laugh."

Though laugh tracks bother him, commercial breaks don't. Jay has no illusions about the bottom-line fact that network TV exists to sell soap. Each episode of *Smoldering Lust* will have two acts, framed by advertising. "My stuff plays better with commercials," he tells Rick and Russ. "Somehow the material needs the break. So do viewers." Clearly he also trusts his audience to stay tuned.

After a couple of weeks of deep talk about the murder and about Chris, Margo, Brodsky, Eve, Cookie, Hal, and Philip, the writers are ready to beat out the next three scripts. The second show, following up on the murder, will be toughest, so Jay takes it. Rick will write the third episode, Russ the fourth. The first episode, still a month away from shooting, remains fair game for everyone. Ideas and notes fly.

Russ: "What about another body in Felton's room?"

Rick: "We could have Cody go so far as to undress in the first show, and as he flees out the door, he drops every form of identification he's got."

Penny: "We'll need an actor with a good body."

Russ: "That's easy."

Jay: "Eve should appear innocent. If she's got any schemes, let's find out about them much later."

Russ: "Let's get Brodsky to show up in the Codys' bedroom when they're both there. At the foot of the bed—or maybe tapping on the window. He needs to talk to both of them. Maybe because he feels for Cody. He hasn't had much experience in this private-eye thing. He's sucked in deep."

Elaine: "Maybe he feels he's getting the couple back together in some roundabout way."

Rick: "We need a place where all the characters can mingle—the office, a restaurant?"

Elaine: "Back in the ballroom?"

Rick: "What if the murderer turns out to be some powerful guy, like a politician. And Cody finds out. They could have some man-to-man talk, Cody knowing the guy's not going down for the crime. And the guy's got something on Cody—not serious, but embarrassing. No police, no evidence, so they work out some kind of justice."

Russ: "We've got to get this murder on the back burner."

And what, the writers wonder, should be said about the inception of the Cody Canyon empire? Is the company the result of Chris's talents or Margo's? Or those of both? It seems important to give some background about Chris and Margo's enterprise. What launched the company—perhaps a revolutionary piece of wilderness gear, like the original duck shoe from L. L. Bean? Russ's suggestion: an "ecologically sound fanny pack." Fanny packs, it is agreed, are funny. "It's what put the Cody company on the map," says Russ. "There's some mythical story behind it. Say Cody was trapped out in the wild and his fanny pack saved his life. Now he demonstrates it—on infomercials?—and it holds a ridiculous number of survival items: knives, compass, dental floss, food, a first-aid kit, a fold-out shield for rain and snow. Somehow it folds up and collapses into micromini size. And maybe it has a one-time use, like an air bag."

After two weeks of discussion the story line of "The Girl in Room 1216" changes little, though the dialogue does go through many revisions. In an early draft a vulgar Brodsky assures Margo that even though her husband is pursuing a gorgeous younger woman, "You're not exactly a bucket of fish guts, yourself." Margo replies: "That's very sweet... and how I hope to be remembered. As not exactly fish guts." In the final version of the script, Brodsky tells Margo, with more grace, that she is a "fine-looking Christian woman." Jay also gives Brodsky hard-boiled lines, the kind of tough-guy talk that makes him seem both cool and jerky at once. "Is she taller than I am?" Margo asks. "She had some height on her," answers Brodsky, trying to sound dispassionate, bored. Margo's simplest question—"What was she wearing?"—gets a smart-aleck response: "Shoes. Skirt. Blouse. Underwear, I assume. But I couldn't be sure." Lengthening the scene by two and a half pages, Jay intensifies Margo and Brodsky's flirtation, revealing more of her anger and desperation. He also shows Brodsky to be nearly incompetent as a private investigator.

In Jay's early March outline for the second episode, heavily scribbled on by Russ and Rick, the tone of the series and the cast of characters are nearly set:

IN. HOTEL/PHONE BANKS—NIGHT 1
Brodsky calls the cops. Reports homicide in room 1216. Gives details, but doesn't reveal his identity.

INT. HALLWAY/ROOM 1216—NIGHT 1
Cops burst into room 1216. Find room empty and clean as a whistle. Brodsky sees the cops leave. "Crank call." He noses around, sees all evidence gone. "Oh, shit." Brodsky wants no part of this. Petty infidelity is fine but murder is too big for him. Felton is hanging around somewhere in b.g. [background]. A marginal note indicates that Brodsky is still in the bellhop disguise he wore in the first show.

INT. PARKING GARAGE—NIGHT 1
Cody and Margo are about to leave event. Cody is trying to pull himself together, just having recovered from passing out.

The next two scenes are crossed out (one has Brodsky avoiding Margo as she and Chris leave the hotel; in the other, Margo and Chris are in a minor traffic accident on the way home, and Hal Kempner comes to the rescue). Jay wrote the first scene to give Brodsky an opportunity to signal to Margo whether or not Chris kept his assignation, but now it seems unnecessary:

better to leave Margo suspicious, uncertain of her husband. "It's enough for us to know that Chris didn't have his tryst," says Russ. "It's okay for Margo to still be uncertain. It'll give her something to confront Chris with later on." As for the second scene, rather than staging a car accident, it's perhaps more effective (and certainly cheaper to film) to have Hal encounter Margo and Chris on foot. He could meet up with the Codys, Rick notes on the outline, "in the parking garage … Maybe Hal lectures them on the virtues of the Toad … Maybe he knows something and alludes to room 1216."

The last scene is a mess. In the first version, a conversation between Margo and Brodsky in Brodsky's record store, the detective tells Margo that he didn't get pictures of Chris and Eve and that she should drop the case; in the second try, the talk is between Margo and her assistant Philip in her office, discussing what might have happened at the hotel the night before. One final attempt goes back to Brodsky at the record store, this time with Cookie, listening to a message from Margo on the answering machine.

The murder is nowhere near being solved, but the character of Cookie begins to take shape as a crack sleuth, far cagier than her boss, with the paranoid streak of a committed conspiracy theorist. Jay's first notion for Brodsky's assistant, that she be a middle-aged woman with a son in college, changes radically into this Cookie: "thirty-five, Asian, [with] a fifteen-year-old kid. She's crazy about Brodsky, hates the record part of the business, loves the private investigating. Keep P.I. focus—she's a people-person. For some reason, Cookie thinks Brodsky owes her big time."

"Because she solved something once?" Russ asks.

"Maybe. She did something for him," says Jay.

The first draft of the third show, Rick thinks, is a "dismal failure." He's beginning to realize just how peculiar the show is, how skewed the sensibility. It will be hard to hire other writers, which they plan to do for the last four or five episodes; at one point Jay asks with dismay, "What if we're the only people on earth who can write these scripts? And what if we're renewed? We'll do nothing for the rest of lives but write *Smoldering Lust!*"

But the more they talk and write, the more Rick relaxes into the job, and the rest of the story outlines are becoming easier. "The rhythm sort of hits you," he says. Part of the difficulty for him at first was not knowing who would play Margo, Chris, and Brodsky. He likes to write with actors in mind—how they move, how they speak. Watching "dailies" (videotapes of the previous day's shooting) will be helpful as the series goes into production, allowing the performers' idiosyncrasies to influence his work. "The tone and the stories are so strange in this series that you really have to get to know the cast a little before you can go very far. You want to make sure the actors can bring off what you're doing."

"When I first read your script," he tells Jay, "I saw the breeziness to it, but there's also that serious core of erotic longing. And if we don't honor that, then the scripts will just seem silly. One of the things we have to do is keep this emotionally real even while everything else gets unreal."

"Such as?"

"Such as the absurd logic of Cody telling his wife, 'Let me sleep with this girl so I can save our marriage.' That's what I mean about being unreal, because it's such a ridiculous thing to say, but also real, because the emotional torment it comes from is genuine. People really do get into these situations."

They talk about sex, about how the show flirts with the dangers of sex. "You know, sometimes you go into a hotel room with somebody and have a great time," says Rick, "and another time just one person walks out. Like Chris does after he finds the dead girl. That weird sense of danger is what sex is about. We've all been through so much sexually, and now how do we close the door to all that? We don't, I guess, and these kind of adult situations are funnier to people who have some experience in the world. The childishness that we've all engaged in, particularly in sexual matters, is funnier at forty, when you're a grown person hurrying out of a room so you won't get caught. In that way, this is a little like a British sex comedy where the adults get in trouble because you don't use your head, you use your heart. You're ruled by lust."

Stabbing at it again, Rick breaks show three into four scenes in two acts. Act I: Record store; Office; Room 1216. Act II: Codys' Bedroom. As Rick beats it out, though, that will change, with the confrontation between Margo and Brodsky in the record store moved to the top of the second act.

The episode opens with Brodsky's telling the audience in one of his signature monologues that he wants off the case: snapping pictures of a guy in bed with someone, that's one thing, but murder—*whoa.* The first act finds Margo in her office, where she is being interviewed. By whom? Visitors? Rick notes. Or a job seeker? A magazine writer? Business students? The office is described as an "open loft space, but there are also places to slip away in secret. This we discover when Margo [happens] upon Cody and Eve."

Chris explains to Eve that they can't pursue one another until the murder is cleared up. Eve seems oblivious to the gravity of the situation, and to the delicacy required in an office romance, and she tries to arrange another rendezvous with Chris. The outline notes, "Eve's motives—her goodness or badness—still are unknown."

The next scene finds Chris, dressed in his trademark outdoor gear—walking shorts, hiking boots, cowboy hat—returning in broad daylight to the hotel. "Self-conscious, trying not to be," he asks the desk clerk obvious questions about the night before: Any unusual sounds from the twelfth floor? Any difficult clean-up jobs there? He proceeds upstairs, where he encounters Felton, who seems to know something ("but let's see here that

Cody trusts Felton"), and the cleaning woman in Room 1216. Desperate, he makes a lunch date with the cleaning woman.

At the top of Act II Margo makes her first trip to Brodsky's record store-office. Now she learns the truth, or part of it, anyway: Brodsky does not have photographs of the assignation because there was none; there was a dead body instead. "This freaks Margo a bit. Her husband was in a room with a stiff?" While this is sinking in, Cookie, looking on, realizes there's something going on between Brodsky and the new client. But Brodsky is spooked and wants off the case. A line is jotted in the margin: "I do insurance fraud and rare records. No murder, no CDs."

Notes scribbled on the third outline raise questions and make suggestions:

> Mention mentality of the 90s—hookers are basically out.
> Eve wants to take "long lunch" with Cody?
> Margo thinks Cody's off to have an affair when he leaves to check on hotel.
> When does Cody realize he's missing something?
> Brodsky shows up in bedroom—"my instincts tell me Cody innocent."
> Felton in gym clothes, or underwear?
> Cody freaked that there's no news of murder.
> Be specific about why Brodsky is dropping case.
> We find out Felton lives in hotel?
> Brodsky will get closer to Margo if he shows he's backing Cody.
> Red herring!

Glad not to have to compete for big laughs, Russ eases into show four. "This town is the way it is," he says, "because a lot of people can sell shit. Even if I know an idea of mine is good I have a lot of trouble selling it to a room full of people. But so many people can push spoiled goods. 'It's set in Chicago, it's about a husband and wife, it's *Seinfield* with Madeline Kahn.' And then once you sell it, you've got to torture it, rewriting and rewriting. Rehearsals are agony because if an actor's not getting giant laughs, the writer pays for it. Good material is thrown out because it doesn't cause a hyena laugh. Actors are always wondering, How many laughs are on this page? How big are they? They get hooked on the size of a laugh! It's why sitcoms get so cartoonish."

Though he knows his way around the big lots—Warner Brothers, Sony, Paramount—he much prefers this no-frills operation, with its lack of a strict hierarchy. At Empire Studios, he finds it remarkable that Jay takes the smallest, least conspicuous office. "And he sits on the floor!" (Jay's motives may have less to do with humility than expediency—in his small back office, he can escape unwanted company.)

Russ's outline of the fourth episode deals more with the characters' inner thoughts than with any particular action.

BRODSKY'S NARRATIVE
    In Felton's room …
    A TV report about body in the Bay
    Pull back to see Felton and [his wife]

ACT ONE
1. RESTAURANT
    Finish damning TV report with "natural causes"
    A waitress remarks about news report
    Then see Cody at table with Bombshell maid
    Cody gently feels her out …
        Any big clean-ups?
        Any stray eyeglass [cases]?
    Bombshell maid thinks Cody's interested in her work
        DISSOLVE TO:
    Later—Maid is still giving history of cleaning solvents.

2. RECORD STORE
   Brodsky looks over glossies of Cody/Bombshell
   Cookie is there.
   Brodsky can't place where he's seen Bombshell
   Cookie helps Brodsky remember.
   Brodsky concludes Margo is married to murderer

3. BRODSKY'S SURVEILLANCE VAN
   Brodsky has asked Margo to join him there.
   Margo's disgusted with van.
   Brodsky tells Margo he thinks Cody's the killer.
   Brodsky—The Voice of Authority
   Brodsky—also lusts for Margo
   Margo asks Brodsky *not* to go to cops.

ACT BREAK

ACT TWO
4. CODY BUILDING—DAY
   Margo is edgy—she talks to Philip about business.
   Hal Kempner shows up to push Toads (suspicious).
      Hal has brought shoes and a flamethrower.
   Margo excuses herself.
   Philip and Hal Kempner together.

5. PHOTO STUDIO
   Margo enters and watches Eve work
   Margo sees in Eve what Margo used to be.
   Margo says something nice to Eve.
   Sad for Margo.

6. CODY BEDROOM—NIGHT
   Margo and Cody in bed together
   She alludes to the murder.

Cody is elusive.
Margo is made hot by the danger of this "murderer."

7. BRODSKY'S SURVEILLANCE VAN—CONTINUOUS
Brodsky listens to them on bugging device.
FADE to Brodsky's Fantasy...
    Brodsky on cover of Cody catalogue.
    Brodsky on bed reading Cody Catalogue.
    Margo appears out of sexy steam.
    Brodsky/Margo make love.
    MUSIC carries into:

8. RECORD STORE—NIGHT
Tight on record spinning
Brodsky's there, alone, listening

BRODSKY'S NARRATIVE.

END

Bouncing off show three, which ends with Brodsky assuring the Codys that he believes Chris is innocent, show four postulates the opposite. If the murder's not going to drag out, why not solve it now? But Russ can't resist implicating Felton in the crime, and further muddies the waters by trying to convince us that Chris is the killer after all. The thematic linking of sex and death becomes explicit when Margo and Chris make love.

The show has two wonderful scenes: Chris's lunch date with the hotel cleaning woman, and Margo's cat-on-a-hot-tin-roof act in Brodsky's van.

Among Rick's and Jay's notes on the script:

Dialogue idea, Cody to maid: "Any unusually big clean-up jobs lately?" Maid's appearance says Fuck Me.

Give Felton quirks—jumpy, ominous, whatever.

Brodsky realizes: Woman he is crazy about is living with a murderer. But we don't need to know his conclusion here.

Margo doesn't believe it, but asks Brodsky not to tell cops. (So she does?)

Cookie's conspiracy theories.

Brodsky wants to be her hero: "There's one person you can trust—me."

We think "Why is Hal doing this? What's his agenda? Not just selling shoes?"

Margo sees in Eve what she used to be when things were good between her and Cody.

Brodsky hears Margo and Chris make love. Then fantasizes about being with her: Brodsky as Cody.

Fantasy: Brodsky in Room 1216, finds supine body—it's Margo. She's alive, they make love. NAW.

In record store, come out with Brodsky listening to melancholy song. Sad, thinking about Margo.

This is where Brodsky falls in love. We see his fantasy.

The scripts pile up and so do the notes. Jay is loath to criticize the work of his two recruits, who have ventured so gamely with him into the warped world of *Smoldering Lust*. "I don't know if my notes are any good," he tells Rick and Russ. "I don't know if they're right, I don't know if what I suggest is funnier than what you've written. I don't know if anything I do is funny." But just as he begins to sound a little desperate, Jay turns acid, the way Rick and Russ prefer him. "But I do have a big house in the Pacific Palisades," he says. "And you don't."

CHAPTER FOUR
A BRODSKY IS BORN

The call about *Smoldering Lust* comes at the right time for Bradley Whitford, just as he returns to New York from a production of *Coriolanus* at the Folger Theater in Washington. It was not a pleasant experience for the actor, who felt it would've been justifiable homicide to murder the director. A graduate of Juilliard, his stage credits include *A Few Good Men* on Broadway and Sam Shepard's *Curse of the Starving Class*. In films he's had small but not insignificant roles—Al Pacino's smarmy nephew in *Scent of a Woman,* Raul Julia's assistant in defending Harrison Ford in *Presumed Innocent.* Bradley's work is fine on screen, but seen in such brief measures, he's not yet a head-turner; audiences haven't left theaters wondering of him (as they did of, say, Brad Pitt in *Thelma and Louise),* "Who *was* that guy?" Fed up with small rewards, joking that he's ready for "more money and less abuse," Bradley has already decided to pursue television offers when, in mid-March, he hears from his agent in Los Angeles, Nevin Dolcefino of Innovative Artists.

When he read the character breakdown on Dave Brodsky he immediately thought of Bradley, and told his colleagues so. "He's the right age, it's his kind of humor. And Jay is one of the best show-runners in the business. He doesn't let anyone else touch the work. Sees it through editing, scoring, everything. This is the kind of television Bradley's been waiting for." Bradley needs to hear this, too; he's pretty new to Jay's work, never having caught

Molly Dodd or more than a couple episodes each of *Slap Maxwell* and *Buffalo Bill*. He has only one hesitation about going up for the part: Can a guy named Whitford play one named Brodsky? "So he doesn't look Jewish," Nevin says. "Neither do I. This the best TV gets, and it's a thirteen-show commitment. There's really no down side. And we can craft a nice deal." Bradley is convinced; he'll go for it. It'll be a long-distance audition, though, so Innovative makes arrangements to put Bradley on videotape in the agency's New York office. "First they fly the tape out," says Nevin. "If they like it, they fly *you* out." The energetic agent's gears have begun to whir.

A high-voltage New Yorker by birth, Nevin grew up in Houston and after taking a degree in European history at the University of Texas stayed on in Austin, writing and performing with a renegade theater group. Moving on to New York, he called a quick halt to furthering his stage career after one embarrassing audition, his first and only, the memory of which still sends him into gales of self-deriding laughter. ("I sang 'Birdland' and it wasn't recognizable," he says. "I'll leave it at that.") To pay his rent, he took a job as a gofer at J. Michael Bloom Ltd., talent, modeling, and literary representatives, and had a fine time darting around Manhattan for the agency. "Who wouldn't? On my twenty-sixth birthday I got to deliver a script to Sigourney Weaver, who was holed up at the Algonquin, hiding from the opening-day craziness over *Alien*." He listened well around the office, quickly learning about client relations and negotiations with casting directors and producers. Though he has never looked back at his flirtation with acting, he values that experience. "I think I'm a better agent because I know what putting on a show entails—and because of my basic love for performers and performing," he says. "There are agents all over L.A. who came up from talent and who became agents just so they could stay close to it. I don't mind admitting that I'm one of them. This business is being taken over by business-school graduates and lawyers. Agents like myself are the last of the breed. We're not even forty years old, and we're the last of the breed. I thrive where I am now, which feels like the center of everything—talent, producing, the business side. It's nice to feel you have some control over it all, especially when you have something people want, like a Brad Whitford. Being an agent incorporates all the things I ever thought I wanted to be—film critic, performer, especially psychologist, since I'm always holding clients' hands."

Eight years after the Bloom agency sent him to Los Angeles, Nevin joined Harris and Goldberg. Founded by Scott Harris and Howard Goldberg and with headquarters in Century City, the dynamic agency is now called Innovative Artists and boasts a richly varied client list: Ann Magnuson, the New York performance artist who made a splash in the Jamie Lee Curtis sitcom, *Anything But Love*; Estelle Getty of *Golden Girls;* and such busy actors as Frank Langella, Jon Tenney, Lou Diamond Philips, and Edward Furlong. Bradley came on board after Howard caught his performance in *A Few Good Men*. Nevin shared Howard's enthusiasm for Bradley and, along with Ken Kaplan and Scott Landis of the New York office, began beating the drums for Bradley. Coordinating his efforts with those of his colleagues, Nevin set out to win *Smoldering Lust* for Bradley as soon as he heard about the show.

The news came from Cheryl Bayer, the freelance casting director hired by Brillstein-Grey to fill all of the show's speaking parts. She is to work with the NBC casting department, which must approve her choices for the lead roles. "Lamb chop!" Cheryl cries over the phone. "I've got something new—it's Jay Tarses, it's thirteen on the air, it's fabulous. Got anybody I should see?"

Nevin loves sending out clients for such shows, and this season he had two to aim for: *Smoldering Lust* and Barry Levinson's *Homicide*. "Certain bells go off when you tell clients it's a Jay Tarses show," he says. "As an agent your brain just clicks. You go, 'I've got to get someone in each of those shows.'" (He does, too:

after booking Bradley and Alison Elliott as Eve in *Smoldering Lust,* Nevin successfully sends Daniel Baldwin up for *Homicide.)*

Bradley had signed on with the agency with the usual caveat about television: "Unless it's something really great, I don't want to do it," and he had already passed on a number of television offers that came his way. But *Smoldering Lust* pricks up his ears: he and the agency agree that this could be career-making. "Visibility is the thing that Bradley needs," says Nevin, "and a good TV show is the best way to get it. There are other ways—an actor could get the same kind of break in the theater, but it would have to be a stunning role in a stunning Broadway play that gets written up everywhere and all the industry people rush to see. But those events are rare. A good part in the right TV show offers incredible overnight visibility, getting the actor's name out there, showing what he can do week after week." Television is also good for actors for other reasons, as Nevin points out to clients. "It's a business that can take care of you," he says. "I don't mean that it's a benevolent industry necessarily, but TV does pay actors well and it's run a bit like the old studios, when actors were kept under contract and coddled a little. Protected. In a sense, networks and the big TV producers can keep actors employed the way that MGM or Paramount or Warner Brothers used to. I like it when my clients can buy houses, raise families."

Innovative is thrilled to have found a showcase for a client whom, as Nevin says verbatim, "we all see tremendous potential in." If only the actor can get the job. Helping the odds is the fact that Jay likes what he knows about the actor, having had a good word from one of his favorite actresses, Megan Gallagher, a co-star of *Slap Maxwell* who is familiar with Bradley's stage work. If the videotaped audition is anywhere near the mark, Bradley will have the chance to improve on it in person. Putting auditions on tape of course saves networks and producers a fortune in making the first cut of hopefuls during casting, but Bernie Brillstein thinks the practice is lazy, even bad for business. "Videotape is ruining the talent-searching process," he says. "It keeps producers and casting people isolated in their offices when they should be out there beating the bushes for actors and comics in clubs and at the theater."

When Bradley reads "The Girl in 1216," he's surprised by how much he likes the script. "I didn't know what to expect. It's actually better than a lot of screenplays I've read." The scene to be taped is difficult, however—the exchange between Margo and Brodsky in the hotel lobby, the "deep-kissing one," as Bradley describes it. Reading Margo's part in the videotaped audition is, according to Bradley, "this casting guy who looks like Fabio. Hairy and muscular." In a cubicle lit by fluorescent lights they begin the furtive love scene. "Kiss me," the Fabio lookalike says, reading off camera. "No—don't touch me." Bradley: "Margo, you're so mercurial—hot, cold, up, down. Baby, get a grip…" The circumstances of the audition couldn't be worse: bloodcurdling screams can be heard from the casting office next door, where auditions for a slasher movie are being held. Certain that he's given a rotten, distracted performance, Bradley shuffled toward home through a light rain. Stopping for a bite in a West Side coffee shop, he almost wishes he could stop the tape from being flown out to NBC in Burbank. "The script was so good," he says, "and what did I make of it? Frogs came out of my mouth. I knew it was over, especially because I went up on tape. You have no control over that—actors know that no one really gives you a chance on tape. They give a few seconds and then hit the off button on the VCR." Bradley fears he'll be zapped with the remote control—just like calling "Next!"

But a day or two later he can't believe what he hears back: the producers want to see him in person.

The following week, NBC welcomes Bradley to Los Angeles in style, putting him up at the St. James's Club, the art deco tower on Sunset Boulevard. He takes in the glamour of the digs: the George Hurrell and Clarence Bull portraits of silver-screen legends, the real potted palms in the dining room and the fake ones around the swimming pool. None of it does much to soothe his nerves about tomorrow morning's audition in Burbank—his first for network television. Bradley has reason to believe that this one will be tough. A Broadway colleague and buddy, Victor Garber, who has already been passed over for the part of Chris Cody, tells Bradley "not to expect them to laugh. They won't laugh at all. They stare at you as if they're wondering what in the world you're doing up there, taking up their time. Don't worry about having what they call a 'good meeting.' Just read, and let them do the talking." The only way Bradley knows to fight audition anxiety is to be a good Boy Scout and be prepared. Back in New York, he has rehearsed the scene again and again with his fiancée, the actress Jane Kaczmarek.

In old Levi's, shirtsleeves, a baseball jacket, and scuffed-up shoes, Bradley takes his rented subcompact from the St. James's Club valet and drives to the audition, fighting job-interview jitters all the way from Hollywood to Burbank. NBC security guards direct him to the third-floor office of network casting director Lori Openden, where Jay jumps up to welcome him and to introduce him to Elaine and Rick, who are sitting on an enormous sofa. Also seated around the bright, spacious room are Kevin Reilly from the drama department and his boss, Warren Littlefield. On a coffee table Lori keeps a big glass jar filled with bite-sized candy bars, but Bradley doesn't notice the rather lame token of hospitality.

Waving a little hello ("Don't make small talk," Jay has warned him), Bradley takes his position in the center of the room, facing an audience that feels more like a jury. He thinks he counts twelve people altogether. Lori will read the part of Margo. *Remember,* Bradley tells himself, *they won't laugh.* The reading begins.

MARGO

What does she look like?

> BRODSKY
>
> She's gorgeous.

> MARGO
>
> I don't mean that. Is she tall?

> BRODSKY
>
> She's got some height on her.

> MARGO
>
> What's she wearing?

> BRODSKY
>
> The usual ...

The thing beyond imagining is happening: snorts of laughter from the assembled casting directors punctuate Bradley's lines, and as the audition goes on, he loosens up, the tension lifting from his shoulders. Afterward, thank-yous and you're welcomes said, he has turned to leave when Lori calls out. "Bradley, wait— can you stay around? We'd like you to read a little more, if you can wait." Out in the reception area he spots another actor, a guy dressed in a suit, who is muttering lines to himself. *Great*, Bradley can't help thinking as his rival is called in—*why didn't I wear a suit?* But when the other actor leaves the casting office he keeps walking, toward the elevator.

Summoned back into Lori's office, Bradley feels like he's among friends and doesn't get rattled even when he blows a couple of lines. From the looks of it, Bradley's Brodsky is dead on.

Later that afternoon, back at the St. James's Club, he gets a telephone call. It's Jay, saying, "You're my choice and I'll do whatever I can to make it happen for you. But they're morons, so anything can happen. Right now it's ninety-seven percent yours."

"So they're still looking?" says Bradley, nervous again, hearing the "ninety-seven" but focusing on the missing three percent.

"Don't worry," says Jay. "Warren just needs to see the tape."

"He didn't see the tape?"

"Apparently not."

Two days later, when Bradley gets word that the job is 100 percent his, he starts making plans to leave New York. Not that he'll give up his rent-controlled apartment on the Upper West Side; like any actor in Manhattan, he knows the move to the West Coast may be temporary, and that he might be back east after making the thirteen episodes of the new series that the network has committed to. He and Jane are glad to make the move together—she also is a client of Innovative Artists—and Bradley's family in Wisconsin is thrilled by his good fortune. "But also a little reserved," says Bradley, whose theatrical debut was an anti-smoking skit he wrote and performed in with the family dog in sixth grade. "Where I come from," he says, "school plays are about as far as anyone goes when it comes to acting. Anything about performing just isn't considered a thing to do with your life. Maybe it has to do with our religion. We're Quakers, and we're not used to it. I mean, we have no production values in our church. Maybe that's why the greatest performers are either Jewish or Catholic."

While packing up for the West Coast, Bradley hears frequently from Jay, who sometimes calls to talk about the show, more often to spar with his new employee, who is fast becoming a friend. Today he offers a theory of why NBC hired Bradley for the part of Brodsky. "Just so you know," he says, "the only reason you got the job is that the network doesn't realize what a big part this is. They're stupid—they think Cody's the lead. They knew I wanted you for Brodsky. And they let me have you, so they can torture me about Cody. 'We'll give you your Brodsky,' they said, 'but now you've gotta do what we say about Cody.' And they plan to force Ryan O'Neal or God knows who else down our throats."

The job means that Bradley can afford to go forth with his marriage plans, which Jay chides him about. "Why do you want to go and do that?" he asked. "That's stupid. If you get married, I promise you two things. One, you will grow to resent each other. Two, you will sleep with other people." He's speaking in jest, but if Bradley hasn't pegged Jay as a total cynic before this, he does now. However the words are meant, their tone is suited to the role Bradley has won and must begin to study: that of a somewhat jaded private detective investigating philandery among the prosperous but bored.

CHAPTER FIVE
FINDING MARGO

L ori Openden keeps a special file in her office at NBC, and when *Smoldering Lust* begins brewing, she is delighted to have a reason to rummage through it. For the past decade, as long as she has headed the network's casting department, Lori has been building a list of actresses with babies or little children. "Just after childbirth," says Lori, "is a very good time to go after an actress with a movie-of-the-week or a series offer. The hours are good, there's usually little location shooting and lots of days off." As soon as she reads the script that Jay submitted to the network in February, Lori realizes she has something to match up with her list when she gets the character breakdown on Margo Cody: "Aware that her husband is about to have an affair, she appears to be having one herself… Nervous, tense, and emotionally mercurial, she appears alternately insecure and outraged … " It sounds like a wonderful part for a mature actress, someone in her thirties. The physical description of Margo in "The Girl in 1216" specifies that she's blond, but the woman Lori is thinking about, whose name she pulls from the Rolodex, has let her hair go back to its natural color. Lori has had her eye on Kate Capshaw since 1978, when the actress made her feature debut in Bruce Paltrow's *A Little Sex,* a New York romance that was only a little funny. At the time Lori was casting a television project for Paltrow and happened to catch the film's dailies one afternoon. *How fresh and attractive,* she thought, watching Kate. "I started thinking then that television would be a good place for her." Now, she says, that's truer than ever: "A woman of Kate's age can get the lead in a good movie-of-the-week. In a feature, she's lucky to get the sixth role, after losing out to Meryl or Glenn." Movie interest in Kate, Lori implies, is now all but over. "I kept an eye on her while it was briefly happening for her in features," she says, referring to Kate's amazing year, 1984, when she opened in four films: *Windy City,* a sweet love story co-starring John Shea; *Best Defense,* an awful, Arab-bashing vehicle for Dudley Moore and Eddie Murphy; *Dreamscape,* a science fiction thriller starring Dennis Quaid; and the big one, *Indiana Jones and the Temple of Doom.* Playing a princessy (and very blond) airhead, an American nightclub singer stuck in Shanghai, Kate has little to do in the movie but shriek in response to the comically male feats of derring-do. But she does so with good grace, and her Chinese rendition of "Anything Goes" that opens the movie proves that she is nothing if not game to go for broke on screen. Ridley Scott's *Black Rain* (1989), a dark, bloody look at organized crime in Japan, gave Kate a neat turnaround from *Indiana Jones,* allowing the actress, by then in her late thirties, to go from shrill to soft-spoken (in English and Japanese), and in low-cut dresses that seemed painted on to show off her voluptuous figure. The film quickly dropped out of sight, however, and when Kate married her one-time director, Steven Spielberg, she happily went into what she calls her "domestic mode…running the very large and complex Capshaw-Spielberg household."

Kate is nursing their third child when Lori starts her search for a woman to play Margo Cody. "Kate's exactly the right age for Margo," she says. "Extremely pretty, but also concerned about getting older. A lady who is starting to age and is worried about that. Looks great in clothes, very stylish. Just like Margo." Just thinking about landing Kate for the role makes her tingle. "I love the idea of engineering Kate's television debut," says Lori.

"There's a lot riding on the leads of romantic comedy, and Kate could be exactly right." She has already rejected a number of actresses in discussions with casting director Cheryl Bayer and the show's producers.

Cheryl, who seems to know what every actor and actress in town is doing at any given moment, gives meaning to her job description by casting what she calls "a humongous net. In meetings I tend to throw out every idea I have, even if I don't totally love them. They just might be interesting. I don't guard my list or keep names to myself. I basically give it away—that's what I bring to a meeting, my knowledge of who's who, who's doing what." Casting meetings for *Smoldering Lust* are lively, with famous and semi-famous names flying around Elaine's office.

"JoBeth Williams?" someone asks, beginning round one of Finding Margo.

"What does she look like now?"

"Not as good as Mimi Rogers?"

"Ooh, but she's a scientologist, isn't she? How can she be funny? People with religion, any religion, are not funny."

"Susan Blakely."

"Good, let's get her to read. Madeleine Smith, too."

"Victoria Principal!"

"For what, *The Victoria Principal Show?* No!"

"Is Ann Magnuson glamorous enough for the network?"

"She's too young for Margo."

"But she's brilliant."

Kate is Lori's idea, and Cheryl likes it. Some other casting directors might have claimed it as their own. "People are always boasting that they've made a great discovery in this business," says Cheryl. "But I'm just glad to hear the right name from someone. Why be competitive? We're all trying to do the same thing, find the best cast possible. A lot of people rush to claim credit when the decision is brilliant, when a great discovery's been made. But the wrong actor is always someone else's mistake."

Lori doesn't like admitting it, but the deciding factor in casting is often how an actor looks, and that secret rule seems especially true of this project. "We don't have a show if the two leads aren't gorgeous," she says. (A talent agent in New York has scrawled across the breakdown sheet for *Smoldering Lust*: GIRLS—LOOK DROP DEAD AT AUDITIONS!) This is one of the hardest comedies Lori has ever had to cast, she says, "because the leads have to be so attractive, and yet funny. We can't have someone who looks like a stand-up comic doing these roles. Funny and not attractive is a lot easier to find—that's why they say that so many stand-up comics are short. I mean, if you look like Tom Cruise or Michelle Pfeiffer, you don't have to be funny."

When Lori mentions Kate, Jay is wary. "But isn't she Mrs. Spielberg?" he says. "I don't want to work with Mrs. Spielberg. She'll expect cars and drivers and a big trailer and things." He's only striking a pose, and Lori says she'll get a script to Kate through her agent at International Creative Management, Tony Howard. "I like doing it myself," says Lori. "Somehow when a script comes from the network, it carries more weight than if it comes from the producers or the show's casting person. It's flattering to the client to know that NBC is actively involved, that the network wants them."

Kate's last word to her agent made her desires anything but clear. "I am only really interested in films," she told Tony. "But don't be shy about sending anything over that you think is worth looking at. Including television." And so on a late March afternoon "The Girl in 1216" arrives at her door in Pacific Palisades. After reading it that evening, she tossed it in the trash.

A few days later, Tony calls. She's keen on the script, and is eager to hear what her client thinks.

"I don't get it," says Kate.

"Then read it again."

"But Tony, I don't even have it anymore. I threw it away."

"So now you can read it again plus two more. I'm sending over three scripts—the first one and the next two."

Kate reads all three and the next day has a friend over for cappuccino. The friend is Sally Field, the actress, who has already read "The Girl in 1216," by now making casual rounds around town, from agent to client to manager to friend; people are reading it just to read it, not necessarily to try out for a part. When Kate complains that she doesn't get the show's attitude, Sally exclaims, "Katie, don't you see? It's funny! You're taking it too seriously!" To illustrate her point, right there in the kitchen she acts out Margo's hotel lobby scene with Brodsky. Sally's opinion counts a lot, coming from someone whose crossover from novelty sitcom star to Oscar winner made Hollywood history. "I didn't have movie idols growing up," Kate says. "I didn't know about Merle Oberon or Katharine Hepburn or Lauren Bacall. I wasn't a movie buff. My role models were Sally and Marlo Thomas." *The Flying Nun* and *That Girl,* she confesses, "helped make me who I am." For Kate, the sense of *Smoldering Lust* begins to sink in: the wonderful confusion of Margo's hot-and-cold feelings for Brodsky, the craziness of her falling in love with the detective she's hired to catch her husband *in flagrante.* She calls Tony back, asking how to proceed.

Have lunch with Jay, she is told.

Low-key doesn't quite describe Kate and Jay's distracted get-acquainted meeting at Toscana, a popular trattoria in Brentwood known for its high noise level and risotto. For a time Jay is more engrossed in trying to fix the wobbly table with a matchbook than in pitching his show, which he does only lamely. "Look, you don't want to do this," he finally tells Kate. "The hours aren't bad, but we're going to do it in the Valley, in Burbank, which is really far from where you live. And it's never going to go past thirteen episodes. It's nothing. You really don't want to do this."

"I know, I know," says Kate, immediately liking the self-deprecating honesty and funny pessimism. An irreverent tone has been struck, and Kate follows through, asking, "So how come no one in this town likes you?" Then she lays it on about Margo: "You know what her problem is? She seems to me like a woman who just needs to get fucked, big. That, Jay, is basically what your show is all about—fucking. Don't you agree?" He laughs, and Kate thinks he's trying not to show that he is a little surprised by the language coming from her, an otherwise so beautifully mannered woman. They laugh much more during what Kate tells him is "a ridiculous lunch that is taking up a lot of my time—I have a lot of errands to run with my kids and you're making me really late." But nothing is resolved when the meeting ends. "We would have had a much better time," says Kate, "if I had just dropped by to get you at your house and let you run errands with me. We could've talked in the car."

Jay is running late too, to meet Rick and Elaine back in Burbank. "Don't worry," says Kate. "Just call them on the way." But he doesn't have a car phone—which is another reason to like him—so she makes the call for him after he speeds off. Neither has any reason to think they'll see one another again.

"I adored it!" she tells her agents at ICM when asked about the lunch. "I love Jay, I'd love to work with him sometime." But for all those fuzzy reasons she and Jay discussed, this doesn't seem to be the right sometime. Nevertheless, Kate thinks a lot about Margo over the next few days, deciding that she must be in love with Chris, no doubt about it, but also wants to jump into bed with Brodsky. No doubt about that, either. She begins to like the role; she especially likes the idea of playing a woman with no children, because, as she says, "my own reality is so inundated with children." Kate has a teenage daughter by her first marriage, and she and Steven have three. She also generously supports the Children's Defense Fund. "I can understand it," she says, "when Margo says, 'I want to adopt a child from a faraway land.'"

But she is torn by indecision. Hearing how much NBC wants her for the part, how much Jay likes her, doesn't make her feel any clearer. It would help if she knew who she'd be playing with, or against, but the part of Chris hasn't been cast yet, though there have been some excited rumbles about Michael Ontkean, and she'd be thrilled to work again with John Shea, who has been asked to read the script. Brodsky is set, but she's never heard of Bradley Whitford and doesn't remember him from *Presumed Innocent* or *Scent of a Woman*. His audition tape is sent over, but she can't tell from it if he's funny or even attractive. And his role, she knows, is crucial: "Brodsky is the show." Fearing the worst about television casting, she sums up the status quo as "bland, oatmeal, mid-America, frightened. They want everyone to look like everyone else. It's all so pitiful."

Agitated, still going back and forth on the project, she finally admits to herself that she is strongly interested, which comes as a surprise to her. "A television series?" she says, "For years, there's been nothing on the air that's made me want to be a part of it or wish that I had done it. That is, until Candice Bergen came along." Could this be, Kate wonders, her *Murphy Brown*?

At her Thursday morning play group—five mothers, nearly twice that number of children—all the talk is about Kate's job offer. Her pals, who are split: two say do it, two say don't. Her teenage daughter Jessica votes yes. "She loves it when I work," says Kate.

When her husband asks her how she's feeling about the project at what Kate calls "reflective, brushing-your-teeth time," she answers, "Like shit." Gathered with friends in her kitchen the next morning, Kate tries to explain her reluctance. She doesn't feel in shape for work—emotionally, mentally, physically. "Careful, Katie," Sally Field had said, voicing her only reservation about the project. "You've just had a baby—you don't want to step back into the business as a plump girl." But apart from all that, Kate is tremendously happy at home, feeling "empowered and effective," she says. "I don't *need* another career. I manage a big family." So she calls Tony at ICM and starts in with her reasons for turning down the role, rambling on about how far away the Valley is, how she's out of shape, the inconvenience of fitting in a job on top of everything else. None of it makes any sense, not even to Kate. She holds the telephone away so that the agent won't hear her cry. "I have to get back to my meeting," Tony tells her. "But if you don't take this, we've got to have a talk."

What about the summer? Kate wonders. She had planned to spend it in East Hampton with the children, while her husband is in Hawaii filming *Jurassic Park*. She could have had the whole summer to get her figure back. But then Jessica leads Kate upstairs for a straight-on mother-daughter talk: "Mom, don't be silly," she says. "Just do it." Almost convinced, Kate calls Steven at his office.

"I just got off the phone with ICM, and I have to take this job. I just have to take it."

"Why are you crying?"

"I'm terrified."

"What of?"

"That I'll be bad."

"Katie, I'm terrified you'll be great."

That does it. He believes in her, her daughter and her friends believe in her. She's ready to go back to work.

CHAPTER SIX
CALLING ALL CODY MEN

Another lead remains open for nearly three months after the start-up of the series. John Calvin gets the call from Bernie Brillstein at the end of May: "I hear you're a good actor," Bernie says over the phone. "Can you act surprised? Welcome aboard!" But John doesn't have to act—he's almost in tears on the floor, a prostrate victor across the finish line. Unlike Bradley's easy sprint to his prize, John has had to hurdle his way through a casting marathon to win the role of Chris Cody. But after the good news comes from the show's producers, the Cody Man—designate hears nothing from NBC. "No flowers, no champagne, not even a congratulations call or note," he says later, still sore from the race.

For the plummy role of Chris Cody, the network first wanted Michael Ontkean, an actor who apparently means it when he says no television for now. John Shea, who was so fine in A.R. Guerney's off-Broadway play *The Living Room,* might have had a ball as super-Wasp Cody, but he turned it down because he didn't like the script, saw little humor in it. The New York stage actor Victor Garber also gave it a go, but he knew he'd lost his chance halfway into his audition at NBC. (It was Victor who told Bradley Whitford not to expect the casting team to laugh during his audition.)

Early on in the casting process, the very mention of Lori Openden's ideal choice to play Chris Cody, Ryan O'Neal, was enough to make wise men and women in the television business shudder. "He's vicious and he's fat," says Jay of Hollywood's oldest bad boy, whose body does indeed seem to have turned into soft ice cream. (Many years of indulgence separate O'Neal from his peak in *What's Up, Doc?* when he could pass for a Chippendale dancer in boxer shorts and a bow tie.) "I know the bad stories about him," Lori countered. She couldn't very well not know after the notorious *Good Sports,* the short-lived ABC sitcom starring O'Neal and his wife, Farrah Fawcett. Cock an ear toward the next table at Patys (sic), Hamptons, or other lunch spots in Burbank and you might still hear one about O'Neal's tantrums and extravagances. According to one observer on the set, O'Neal, after repeatedly flubbing a line containing the words "murder," "maybe," and "mother," exploded, screaming at the writers, "You motherfuckers are trying to fuck me up with too many fucking *m* words!"

But Lori wanted still O'Neal for Chris Cody. "I really like him," she says. "He's funny, and though he *is* too heavy right now, he's still attractive. In the right situation it would work—I'm hopeful we'll find the show for him." But it won't be *Smoldering Lust,* not when Cheryl Bayer has anything to say about it. Cheryl took the side not only of Jay but also of Bernie Brillstein (who produced *Good Sports)* and Russ Woody (who worked as one of the show's writers): "If you're talking seriously about Ryan O'Neal, I'm out," she said in an early casting meeting. "That would change the whole nature of the show." (She felt the same way about an early notion to offer the role of Margo to Victoria Principal. "No," she said adamantly. "The show I signed on for is classy. Why trash it?") If NBC insisted on O'Neal, she adds, she'd quit. When the subject of temperamental actors comes up, Lori quotes her former boss Brandon Tartikoff: "He once said to me, 'If we only hired actors who didn't have problems, we'd have entire nights of zero programming.'" Maybe so, but this team is determined not to add stars' egos to the usual problems that beset a production. "It's us against them," Cheryl told her cohorts afterward. She counted the meeting a success when NBC backed away from O'Neal.

Back at square one, Cheryl decided to fight for John Calvin. Everyone in the business knows the name of this busy actor, whose credits read like a choice listing in TV *Guide,* from *Mike Hammer* to *L.A. Law.* He co-starred with Bette Davis in a 1978 movie-of-the-week called *The Dark Secret of Harvest House,* and with Don Johnson a year later in a miniseries based on *From Here to Eternity.* John's feature film roles include the hard-line factory foreman in *Norma Rae,* and he feels he's played too many heavies over the years: "corrupt cops, unscrupulous politicians, abusive boyfriends, insensitive husbands, dishonest witnesses— dog kickers, in general." One of his few sympathetic roles comes in the last reel of *Making Love,* as Michael Ontkean's lover, and he is eager for an imagesoftening role again. To Cheryl's mind, John has just the right sensibility for Chris, but Lori doesn't agree. She's known John a long time and likes him fine, but "in support-ing roles; I've never seen him as the star of a show." Certainly the actor fits the description of the Cody Man she rattles off in cast-ing meetings: "Tall, well built, with a full head of hair, someone who looks great in clothes." But it's hard to be handsome and funny, Lori believes—forgetting, perhaps, about Cary Grant in *The Philadelphia Story* and *Bringing Up Baby,* or, for that matter, Ryan O'Neal in *What's Up Doc?* The point, she insists, is that the new series is "funny in a different, difficult way," and the actor who plays Chris, she tells agents around town, "has to be funny with a twist. We're looking for someone whose brain reacts in a different way, who can get on the *Smoldering Lust* wavelength." Such exclusivity at least makes it easy to eliminate lots of actors— "One line into the audition and you just know if they get it." Also complicating the search is the character's age. Actors in their twenties seem to be in abundance and, still young, have not been pounded into comedic or dramatic niches. "It's tough trying to find someone good-looking who's also got that twist, *and* is in that age group. You either have to go for a star—a Ted Danson or a Patrick Swayze or if we possibly could a Tom Hanks—or you take a chance on someone who's been around awhile and is just now getting a shot at a lead. Like a John Calvin."

John first hears about the job from his agent, Scott Manners, who runs his own talent agency out of a bungalow off Sunset Boulevard. "You're perfect for it," Scott tells his client, eager to see him as a romantic lead. "This'll get you away from playing villains. And it's an attractive deal—if it works out you'll be busy all summer. They're shooting thirteen. Interested?" The male lead in a network comedy? A thirteen-episode guarantee? Of course John is interested, but after reading "The Girl in 1216," he wants to know what gives with Chris—does he love Margo or not? He has no reservations about the material, however, which he compares to "a little jewel of a feature film." The job is a shot at what his agent calls "Ted Danson Land."

John arrives at Empire at four o'clock on the afternoon of April 16 to read for Jay and Cheryl. He has prepared three scenes, with Cheryl reading Margo's part, but the first two play so well, to such easy laughter, that he looks up and asks if he should continue. "Nah," says Jay. "Quit while you're ahead." The reading at Empire surely is good enough to get a network audition and for nearly three weeks John waits for the call. Finally on a sunny May morning he strides into Lori's office—and John's are very long, purposeful strides. His "Hi! How are you?" does nothing to soften the stares of those seated at the long, curved sofa like, he later says, a "silent Greek chorus." The reading goes well. Cheryl pronounces him "our Cody." Jay and Rick like the way he has underplayed the humor and toys with the character's befuddlement. But Lori wants the words to fly off the page, as they say in Burbank, and she can't see or hear that happening. She also has doubts about the romantic tension with his leading lady. She wants fireworks, yearning to recreate the Sam-and-Diane dynamite of *Cheers,* which she considers "the best chemistry ever on television—and no one knew it until the show was up and going." That experience taught her two rules of casting: to choose carefully, however long the search drags on, and then to wait and see—give the actors time to hit the right notes. That special TV magic, she thinks, will spark Helen Hunt and Paul Reiser on the new series she has just cast, *Mad About You,* and she'd love to make it happen again with the actors who win the roles of Margo and Chris Cody.

Shuddering at the memory of the "blood-chilling" auditions, John visits his agent a few days afterward for some bucking up and hand holding. Trying to be reassuring, Scott gives him his standard speech about the downturn in business all over town— "Don't take it personally, it's not *you.* Lots of actors are looking for work right now"—when a call comes in from Lori. Impulsively, Scott switches on the speaker phone as she breaks the news: "We think we have to move on, Scott. We just don't see how we can make this work with John. Warren doesn't think he can carry a series." John is crushed. "I know it seems odd sometimes when we pass on someone," Lori continues. "It's tense and painful, but we do have reasons. Networks just do things differently— not necessarily right or wrong, just different." It is perhaps the most awkward moment of John's still young career, to be sitting in his agent's office and overhear the verdict against him. "What is their problem?" he wonders, putting the question to Jay, who reassures the actor, telling him that the network's decision is not necessarily final, and that he's "not expected to carry the series. This is an ensemble piece. Stop torturing yourself. Don't take on more responsibility than you're supposed to."

For all the hocus-pocus about chemistry and sparks, John suspects he knows what his problem is: low Q. The idea of "Performer Q," a numerical measure of an actor's popularity and the public's familiarity with him or her, was originally devised by a Long Island-based consulting firm called Marketing

Evaluations. Q scores are extrapolated from mail-order questionnaires sent out to some 7,200 households that are demographically matched to current census data, and the results are published annually. According to the survey for 1992, the ten most recognized and liked performers in the United States were Bill Cosby, Michael J. Fox, Clint Eastwood, Katharine Hepburn, Paul Newman, Robin Williams, Estelle Getty, Carol Burnett, Tom Selleck, and Betty White. John Calvin doesn't know for sure what his ranking is—other than releasing the names of the top ten for promotional purposes, the research company guards its surveys, charging some $20,000 for the published results—but he is fatalistically certain it's near the bottom. "I've got low Q," he laments. "Audiences get me mixed up with other actors. Or they don't like the characters I play. And the networks use that against me. It's a vicious cycle, too, because the thing that would raise my score, a regular role on television, is exactly what you can't get if you have low numbers. It's like any job, where you can't get hired if you don't have experience—but then how else do you get the experience?"

But miraculously, Q rating be damned, it starts to look as though John might get the job. In early May the network calls Scott Manners, who immediately rings his client at home: "It's alive! Be prepared to read again tomorrow. They want to put you on tape." A messenger arrives with pages for a new scene—Chris and Margo this time, half naked in the bedroom, he looking preoccupied while she tries to seduce him. Like a student cramming for an exam, John calls his girlfriend, asking her if she can spend the evening running lines with him. They rehearse into the night.

Two weeks before shooting of the series is to begin, John goes on tape. He's still fighting the creeping feeling that he's the network's "insurance man—a fallback if they can't find anyone else." His line reading and the attitude he gives the character are fine, he thinks; he's worried about his appearance: How will he look on tape? Should he have shaved his beard? Is his denim shirt too dark? A day later Elaine Arata is a bit chagrined to report that the network executives, after viewing the tape, are still looking. "I don't know who else they're calling," she says, "but we still want you very much. All of our eggs are in one basket, and it's you." When word arrives that Kate has been cast as Margo, John knows his agony can't last much longer; filming is scheduled to start on June 10. He hardly hears Scott's voice advising him to stay close to the phone. "We'll know one way or another within hours."

When the call comes, John doesn't recognize Bernie's name, but it doesn't matter; all he hears is "Welcome aboard." With less than a week to get his Cody Man act together, John must forgive and forget the bruising casting process he's endured, a bloody one even by Burbank standards. He tries not to sound petulant when he reviews the ups and downs of the casting procedure. "I don't take it personally. What happened to me was that I just saw more of the horror than an actor is supposed to see. But I understand now why so many performers become assholes."

CHAPTER SEVEN
THE LOOK OF LUST

Imagine *Double Indemnity* or *The Maltese Falcon* in color. That's what *Smoldering Lust* aspires to look like, with a subdued palette of smoky rooms, moonlit scenes, late-afternoon sun slanting in through french doors.

The company is off to a late start this morning. At seven-thirty Lesli Glatter, who is directing the scene in episode five where Chris meets Eve in a seedy motel room, announces first thing that she doesn't like the way the walls look. "Great color," she says to art director Ann Champion, indicating the intentionally yucky expanse of yellowish brown. "But it's not grungy enough. This is supposed to be a dive, the Bates Motel almost." It's an appropriate reference from someone whose directing credits include four episodes of *Twin Peaks*. Lesli's criticism sends Ann spinning. Racing into her office, she reaches for the fix-all that no budget-minded art director goes without—Streaks & Tips hairspray, the kind beauty suppliers sell (FOR EXTRA-FIRM HOLD AND QUICK COLOR TOUCH-UPS, the label reads). Back on the set, now teetering on a ladder, then on her hands and knees, Ann "knocks down" the wall, applying the look of years of wear and grime with every *pssst* from the aerosol can. *Pssst*, onto doorjams and around doorknobs, light switches, window frames. *Pssst*.

Ann has been in crunchier spots than this in her career; once, on a location shoot, she executed a quick aging with a vile mixture of soy sauce and coffee, begged from the catering truck.

But she hates doing this sort of last-minute fix with the crew standing around fidgeting. "It looks like I haven't done my job," she says. "But all I'd heard until this morning was how terrific the set looked, that we were ready to go. This is upsetting because we're holding up production and even though it's no one's fault, everyone's thinking, They're having to fix the set right there in front of the camera. That's the worst thing an art director or production designer can do—fix the set in front of the camera. This is not how I wanted to start the day."

Jay takes advantage of the down time to drop by hair and makeup for a free trim from Diane Biggs. As soon as he's seated Ruth Bracken, the set decorator, pokes her head in the doorway. "The boss is strapped in a chair," she says. "Captive audience." She's got an idea for Eve's apartment described in Rick's outline for episode six as "a simple, low-rent two-bedroom apartment that a college sophomore would be proud to call home for a couple of semesters. Not pay-by-the-hour, but close." Eve shares the drab flat with a surly young man named Billy, who, we learn from their first snappy exchange, is her roommate only, not her lover. All the elusive Billy ever does is quarrel with Eve, munch on popcorn, and watch television. Ruth has been digging through the script for more clues, trying to figure out how to dress the apartment.

A few lines of dialogue imply that Billy, amazingly enough, is rich, from an inheritance or winning the lottery or something else that required no talent or effort on his part. If Billy's got so much money, Ruth wonders, why not get him some fancy toys? "We know he loves television," she says to Jay. "All day he's there on the sofa, glued to the set, a TV addict. So let's fill the apartment with television sets, but really fill it—old ones, new ones, huge sets, little portables. It'll be like a showroom, except that there'll be vintage models too." The idea at first strikes Jay as a cluttered sight gag, and he groans. But Ruth persists: "The sets won't get in the way of the scene, I promise. It's not like they'd all be turned on—he only watches one. But visually, they're interesting." Realizing she's not going to drop it until he okays the idea, Jay does so.

Though Ruth has opened accounts at prop shops all over town, she strikes a deal for the TVs with one, Lennie Marvin's. Ruth's allowance for rentals is $4,000 a show, a paltry sum to furnish and decorate three permanent sets plus a half-dozen temporary ones. Prop shops like Lennie Marvin's are hangarsized and organized along the lines of a theme park: the American West, Chicago in the thirties, Suburbia 1950, the Antebellum South, the World of Tomorrow. Jammed with furniture, appliances, decorative objects, even brand-name products from decades past, prop shops are like Smithsonian emporiums. Ruth starts her collection with a Westinghouse made of gray plastic, equipped with its own leggy stand. She also gets a console with a mahogany-veneer, Motorola's "Mediterranean," and a novelty model that's simply a tube perched above speakers shaped like jet engines. By the end of the week she's stacked about two dozen TVs into Billy and Eve's apartment, a temporary set that will be struck next week, turning it into the wacky showroom of her dreams, one that says something interesting about the character who occupies it. The collection of televisions may in fact be the most remarkable thing about Billy, a nebulous character who disappears from the show after Eve moves in with Margo in episode ten. Billy is the thinnest of dramatic characters, not just illuminated but fleshed out by set dressing.

Ruth has been decorating and designing stages since 1983, when she first teamed up with art directors at Southern California advertising agencies to produce television commercials. Her first print campaign, for Mattel toys, was followed by one for lingerie. Remarking that "you can't afford to specialize in this business," she has done ads for Clorox, Miller Lite, American Savings Bank, Clusters cereal, and Mercury minivans. "Creating a handsome bar for a bottle of beer or a background to showcase a shiny new car—that's the kind of thing I did." Still does, too, when feature and TV jobs don't come through. A single mother of a ten-year-old son, Ruth has to keep working; as soon as one project ends, out go the telephone calls, résumés, and reels. When *Smoldering Lust* ends, she will begin dressing a warehouse in East L.A. for a horror film skeletally budgeted at $1 million. Though grateful for the work, she recalls similar jobs and can't say she's looking forward to this one: "All you can do is move things around to make it look like you have more furniture than you do, try not to get killed, and add up numbers."

Ruth holds a degree in theater arts from the University of California at Berkeley, and another in landscape architecture from UCLA. Graduating in 1968, she moved to New York to study dance, though not with any real desire for a career. The training shows, though, in her erect posture and in her lean, strong body (she rarely asks for help moving heavy pieces of furniture around on a set). Blond and tanned and fond of long skirts, boots, beads, and vests, she is the sixties-era ideal of the California girl. Her leap from landscape architecture to interior design came naturally. "I think a designer is a designer," she says, "whether it's rooms, landscapes, houses, furniture, flower arrangements. A good designer should be able to design anything."

Her job at Empire rivals Lani Reynolds's in the wardrobe department for time spent shopping, though scavenging and scrounging more aptly describes what Ruth and Lani do. Commiserating about their budget woes, the two joke that they've cried more on this production than on any other. "We cry between stores," says Ruth, laughing. "Stuck in traffic, desperate to find affordable things, we sob." Furnishing the lives of this show's characters requires great familiarity with the likes of Conran's and Ikea, Pottery Barn and Pier 1, Macy's and Linoleum City as well as dozens of hole-in-the-wall secondhand shops. Often Ruth hits the stores late, after work, and just as often she's out of the house early. Once a week she makes a pre-dawn raid on downtown L.A.'s immense flower market.

Ruth was hired at the beginning of May by the production's original art director, Jim Dultz, with whom she had worked briefly before on a restaurant interior. Their collaboration didn't last long this time either. "A few days after we got going," Ruth says, "I walked in and Jim said, 'Meet my replacement.' It was Ann." Dultz's departure was amicable, and in any case Ruth and Ann had no time to fret over it, not with just four weeks to pull together three permanent sets, from blueprints to curtains—the Cody Canyon offices, the Codys' bedroom, and the record store.

"You don't stop during preproduction," says Ruth, tapping the steering wheel of her sea-green Honda Accord. Traffic on Highland is backed up between Sunset and Santa Monica, just as she is scrambling to put the finishing touches on Brodsky's record store. Creeping down the avenue, she hears her beeper, checks it, and reaches for the phone. "Ralph? Ruth Bracken. Fine, just stuck in traffic. Feels like ninety degrees. I'm in the car, so talk to me." Ralph Fowler, from Hollywood Studio Gallery, has provided most of the artwork for the sets, and he'll be getting back to Ruth about posters for the record store. "We don't need them today," Ruth tells him. "Just soon. This is a permanent set, so we can keep adding to it all summer. As they come in, tag them for us and call me. Remember, this is for a funky old record store in San Francisco." Throughout the four-month shooting period, Ruth will pile on the details in Brodsky's shop, bringing in more posters as she finds them, along with lamps, fabrics, more record albums. For most of the next four months she'll keep an eye out for the kind of things Brodsky would surround himself with.

Like the Ricardo living room in *I Love Lucy,* the record store is probably the most important set in *Smoldering Lust,* and it isn't easy to get right. Because of the way Brodsky comments on the action directly to the audience, viewers must feel comfortable in his domain. BRODSKY'S USED AND DIFFICULT-TO-LOCATE 331/3 RECORD SHOP AND DETECTIVE AGENCY is now sketchily hand-painted on the door, replacing the press-type lettering that Jay deems too neat. He's also given a few pointers for fixing up the record shop in marginal notes to the story outline of show two: "No CD's, no 8 tracks, please. LP's only. You have to go down a few steps from the street to get here. It's cluttered, musty and cramped. LP records are all over the place. There might be a filing system, but it's in somebody's head. If you worked here... your job wouldn't be easy to describe. You sort of do whatever's needed and you have to roll with the punches."

For two weeks Ruth has been amassing treasures for the two-level set, which consists of stairs leading down from what's meant to be a dim San Francisco street and a large room where Brodsky's disheveled office (wooden desk, black rotary telephone, oscillating fan, lean-back arm chair) shares space with the low-rent retail operation (crates and shelves packed with records, a cash box). The walls are ochre; projected onto them are slashes of sunlight that pierce the room through venetian blinds (an effect created by placing a louvered panel over a lamp). A raveled braided rug covers part of the concrete floor. An LP spins on a turntable circa 1959. Hanging on wall pegs are dozens of records in black, red, and blue vinyl (rented by the pound from Lennie Marvin's). Aficionados will gasp—no collector would ever expose vinyl platters in this way—but it's otherwise a fine piece of work, this moody grotto of a set.

The day before shooting begins, though, stepping up on the stairs to survey the room, Jay tells Ruth he's not completely happy with it. "It's not there yet. It's a little too much on the poor side. Too downscale. Brodsky's not quite this bad off. Can you bring it up a little? There's just not enough comfort going on in here." For the first time, Ruth looks at the set for the other function it's supposed to fill: this is also where Brodsky lives. "You want it homier?" she asks. Jay wants to know what it would take to "fill the place up." A thousand bucks, she thinks, but the figure she gives is only a fraction of that; the problem is nothing a little shopping can't fix. It has to be warp-speed shopping, though: the camera will roll at three tomorrow afternoon.

On the way home that evening, driving from Burbank to Venice, Ruth stops at Conran's for rugs. Spotting two she likes, a dark-blue sisal and a coral-and-green cotton, she decides on the cotton, writing a check for $64 plus change. One item off the list, she's got a jump on tomorrow. By nine the next morning, she's at Pier 1, piling up black-and-white throw pillows at a cash register. She buys six. A low pine table with ornate legs catches her eye. "I'd love to gild the legs and marbleize the top—make it into a treasure Brodsky might have found on the street." But there's no time for that.

Her car trunk and backseat now crammed, Ruth turns north toward Burbank and makes a quick stop for posters at The Record Collector near Santa Monica Boulevard. The shop could have inspired Brodsky's place, with its atmosphere of musty chaos: records crammed into floor-to-ceiling shelves, album covers scattered on the floor (Lionel Hampton, Stan Getz, Peggy Lee, Billie Holiday, Dave Brubeck, Ella Fitzgerald). There are no posters, though. "Other places get them before I do," says the near-sighted man minding the store. "Try Larry Edmunds." Ruth has already thought of the store on Hollywood Boulevard, just down from Grauman's Chinese, next to Frederick's of Hollywood. The temperature is rising and she's pushing noon, but Ruth risks one more detour.

Larry Edmunds Cinema and Theatre Bookshop is a New Yorker's bookstore, overstuffed and almost overstaffed, crowded with buyers, not just browsers. In addition to its enormous inventory of theater and film books there are thousands of movie posters. Ruth finds two that will do, for *Pete Kelley's Blues* and *Round Midnight*. The clerk encourages her to check back.

Persistence pays, as she knows from her earlier quest for a saxophone to hang in the shop. "You'd think there'd be plenty of saxophones lying around L.A.," Ruth says back in the car, heading to the studio. "But musicians are competing with me. I struck out everywhere and finally tried a pawnshop in Hollywood. No luck, but the man there said to try again, something was sure to come in. I did try, three times, and finally he brought out this beauty. But there was a catch—he said it belonged to someone who was wanted by the police. 'The owner's on the lam,' he told me." Ruth begged and badgered him, hoping he'd take up the matter with the police. He did, and Ruth got the sax—after putting up a couple hundred dollars as a kind of bail, and by signing a promise to return the instrument if the police need it. "It's a gamble," she says. "We could lose a nice prop. I'm keeping my fingers crossed."

The morning shopping spree pays off: with the rug, the pillows, and the posters, Brodsky's shop, still plenty bohemian, is homier than before. As a rule, Ruth pays no mind to what actors have to say, but she is pleased to overhear Bradley telling others on the set how good it looks.

Talking about the Codys, Ruth sounds like a real-life interior designer, sizing up new clients, trying to second-guess their likes and dislikes. "Margo and Chris are opposites," she says, seated in her tiny office at Empire, which is dimly lit with a single green-shaded desk lamp. She is reviewing yet another shopping list, this one for the Codys' cabin. "Chris is passive about everything, including the way their home looks. Whatever Margo wants, he goes with. He's hard to figure out. I do think he has good taste, but it takes Margo to bring that out." Ruth has read only the first few scripts, but her hunch is correct—a flashback episode late in the series will reveal that it is indeed Margo who takes Chris's instincts and runs to market with them. "If Cody is aware of anything about his surroundings at home or at work, it's what they convey, the image they project." The list of items for the cabin is complete: camp blankets, Navajo rugs, western-motif sconces, knickknacks made of birch bark, an Adirondack chair.

Reading a script for the first time, Ann Champion's chief concern as art director has to do with the spatial restrictions and requirements of the camera. "I can build the best-looking set in Burbank," she says, "but it won't matter unless the director of photography can get the camera in to film it." Arriving at every production meeting with rough floor plans, Ann huddles with Steve Confer, the D.P., and the episode director to block out scenes. Discussing Eve and Billy's at-home encounter, the humor of which hinges on Eve's awkward comings and goings from the kitchen and on Chris's unexpected arrival at the front door, Ann and Steve thrash out design issues: How should the kitchen door open? Where should the front door be? Can the sofa face the kitchen? Should daylight show from a window? Where can the camera dolly tracks be laid?

Ann's background is in theatrical scenic design (she has admired Jay's work since her days at Southern Methodist University, when she noticed his name among the writing credits for *The Bob Newhart Show).* Assisting on *Cagney and Lacey, Parker Lewis*, and other shows, she's been surprised to discover that television demands so much of her skills in making audiences suspend disbelief. "Theater audiences are so clearly on the outside looking in, and they expect to see a make-believe world," she says. "But people seem to think that television is utterly real, that we're actually part of their living rooms. Television puts them so directly into the action that I feel enormous pressure to make it all seem totally believable." What Ann misses about the theater are the hours. "I'm nocturnal," she says, yawning over a cup of early-morning coffee in the Codys' bedroom. "Late hours suit my body clock a lot better than this." Most mornings Empire Studios is in full swing by seven o'clock—hammers banging, computer keyboards clicking, actors sleepily drifting into the makeup room.

Ann is on hand along with her assistant, Lori Rowbotham. Though her job is technically completed once the camera starts rolling, it is understood that the art director must be first on the set every morning, a point of etiquette referred to as "opening up the company." The practical considerations behind the tradition are real. "You don't know what the set's going to look like until the lights are on it and you're looking through the camera." Production may appear to stop for nothing once it starts, but that's not always true; it often makes sudden pauses for fixes like that necessitated by Lesli's last-minute objection to the motel-room walls. "It's a drag, but you deal with it," says Ann. Even visitors to a set, she's learned, hold strong opinions about how a show should look, and they aren't shy about offering them. "Art direction and production design seem to be in the public domain," she says, smiling politely and saying thank-you whenever an actor, a script supervisor, an assistant director, a gaffer comes to her with suggestions. If the criticism comes from the director or the director of photography, however, she acts quickly.

Ann and Lori share an office just off the stages. Each has her own drawing table piled with sketches. The reference books lying about are guides to the *Smoldering Lust* milieu: *Grand Hotels of the World, American Log Homes, Adirondack Furniture, Illustrated Catalog of Victorian Plumbing Fixtures, Trademarks of the 40s and 50s, San Francisco's Heritage in Art Glass.* Also piling up are scripts and story outlines, which Ann and Lori must read in order to plan for all the sets needed, since they aren't able to do anything until they know where the stories are going. The Codys' wilderness cabin is first mentioned in an outline to show twelve as being "simple and rugged, except [with] the accoutrements necessary for survival in the nineties—a cappuccino maker and a Stairmaster and maybe a TV." Drawing up floor plans, Ann and Lori sketch a loft area for an office, an open kitchen, a large hearth. The cabin, which was Margo and Chris's first love nest, is a funny counterpoint to the their bedroom, showing how their relationship and way of life have evolved.

At home in San Francisco, Margo and Chris still share a bed, but they sleep back to back, facing away from one another. The writers lavish specifics on the Codys' bedroom, stipulating in outline notes that it be "large, comfortable, with a dressing room, a bathroom off to the side, and a brick terrace... An intimate French country room... probably on the third floor of a townhouse in downtown San Francisco." As the bedroom is being built, Jay encourages Ruth to think of it as Margo's lost romantic ideal. The bedroom is important not just because it is "where Margo and Chris spend most of their time," as Rick Dresser notes in an outline to show three, but because it's all we ever see of their home. Jay insists that the bed be a king-size four-poster; it is a crucial piece of set dressing, the site of passion lost. "Think sex," he tells Ruth. "Seduction." For three full days, Ruth looks at beds, snapping pictures in department stores, outlets, and antique shops. "I think I've photographed every bed in Los Angeles," she tells Jay, showing him the pictures of what they agree are slim pickings. None of the candidates seems right, and Ruth decides to have one custom-made. She's already contacted an ironworks in La Brea called Relic, which will do the job for $1,800. The next day Ruth delivers a sketch for the iron-frame bed, its slender posts rising up to form a canopy.

When the bed arrives at the studio, Ruth is ready with a thousand dollars' worth of linens, including gauzy white drapery for the canopy. Ready for a princess and her knight, the bed is impossible for the camera and viewers to ignore. For the crew, however, the bed is a pain. Steve has trouble getting the camera around the posts to peek through the drapery, and the canopy discourages aerial shots. "It's a bird cage," he says. It also requires difficult maneuvering by the sound team. Lowering the long arm of the boom mike through the canopy and holding it at awkward angles, Gillian Childers struggles to get close enough to the actors without smacking into the iron posts.

Ann and Ruth work for the director, and director of photography, not the actors, so it doesn't matter to them that Kate Capshaw hates the bedroom, calling it "the creepiest set I've ever been on. You see the lack of warmth that's the backdrop of their marriage, the bed that they're not making love in." The set may be an accurate reflection of the Codys' marriage, but elsewhere "Margo has much stronger, simpler tastes than you see in the bedroom. Look at her office, with the exposed brick walls, unfinished wood, sensible furniture. Wouldn't she have the same look at home?"

The fairy-tale bed, however, suits the room that Ruth and Ann have created. There are also a delicate lady's desk, a slipper chair upholstered in a flowery fabric, a feathery palm tree in a Chinese pot. There are tapestries, two after Fragonard's rococo paintings *Oath of Love* and *Two in Ecstasy in Garden,* depicting courtiers romping, ladies soaring skyward on swings, bosoms heaving. Even the fireplace screen bears a sweet image of two plump cupids tending a fire. Does Barbara Cartland live here? If she'd had the budget to do so, Ruth would have added one more piece, a bronze nude of entwined lovers. Above the fireplace is a witty reminder of the consequences of lust, a barebreasted woman surmounted by demons. Books atop Margo's nightstand include a novel entitled *The Ragged Way People Fall Out of Love* and two self-help volumes, *Composing a Life* and *Learned Optimism.* Chris's shorter stack reveals his sensitive, politically correct side: *Iron John* and *Lessons of the Rainforest.*

Kate may be right that the bedroom gives an overly soft impression of Margo as a woman too vulnerable and too idealistic, but the set's excess does mirror the desperation she feels in love. In this doily of a room Ruth has created, Margo is not the confident woman she is on the job (where she flatly declares, "I'm in control") but rather is reduced to asking her husband, "Why can't you just look at me?"

Show thirteen is set in the Codys' cabin, which Lori makes a 3-D model of, in white cardboard. With a budget per show of about $12,000, Ann is worried about the cost of building it: "Whoever came up with these figures hasn't been to a lumberyard lately." Another $4,000 an episode would give her breathing room. But she knows the show's budget woes aren't unique, not in the 1990s. "We're in the same bind as everyone else. Unless you're in the top ten shows, they want you to do it for free. Vendors all over town are compromising, taking less, pinching pennies. It's just what you do now if you want to work."

Ann has been terribly hampered on *Smoldering Lust* by mistakes made before her arrival, when a set services company, originally hired to build the three permanent sets for $120,000, overspent by $45,000. Pointing out that she could have gotten the job done for $100,000, she fired the first crew. "I don't like set services generally," she says. "They're expensive, partly because we have to pay for their overhead." The work, she adds, is sloppy: walls designated on blueprints as "wild"—that is, removable—were nailed down, and she had to undo the damage.

She did so by hiring Mike Wright, a freelance construction coordinator, whose work is regularly on time and underbudget. "He saved us," she says. "I've always made a point of having good crews, but this one is extraordinary. He and his guys work really hard to make this show happen. They even bring in tools from home, or they call friends at studios for loaners and freebies." Mike spends a lot of time chugging figures into his calculator. "Either side can get me. If I'm not delivering the look they want, I answer to Art. If I go over budget, the production manager speaks up." Twice during the production of this series he will have to lay off his crew of six in order to make the budget. Still, he and his crew—five men, one woman—are glad for the sometimes erratic employment. "There's not a lot of work out there right now. And not big pay when you do get it." With the economy depressed and production pinched all over town, Mike can only daydream about his lucrative days on *Tango & Cash,* when he had a crew of 250 men and women. "We spent three hundred fifty thousand bucks in two weeks," he says. "Unbelievable." Now, his low-as-he-can-go quotations for his work on *Smoldering Lust* must cover his own salary, wages for his crew, shop rental, telephone expenses, even trash removal.

When a decision must be made about whether to build a set or go on location, Ann often has a swing vote. Though a location may be perfect for visuals and atmosphere, she knows that some places are simply too much trouble. "I'm concerned about the restaurant scene," she tells Steve and Jay as the crew gears up to film show ten. "It's seven or eight pages of dialogue—a lot of talking, a lot of over-the-shoulder shots. It might go more smoothly if we build rather than go on location." But Jay doesn't like the idea. He wants a real restaurant, real backgrounds. Liz Matthews, the location scout, has found one in the valley that will let them take over for two days. Visiting it herself, Ann blocks out the scene with Steve, who wants a couple of booths removed. That shouldn't be a problem, Ann thinks, as long as Ruth can camouflage the damage. He also wants a wall built to enclose two sides of the table where the four actors will sit. Ann makes a sketch. A half-dozen crew members are all over the place, measuring, eyeballing the space, moving furniture around. After an hour, the word is go: they've come to the right place.

The company also goes on location to film a jacuzzi scene for show nine, and Ann pitches in to give the place the look of a tony men's club. Filmed in a generic-looking Marriott hotel in Woodland Hills, the setting lacks elegance, and to fix that she wants to install tile walls. Tiles, however, are expensive, and so is the labor of the people who lay them. So she dashes over to Home Depot to buy a piece of fake tile wainscoting for $25. Set up around the jacuzzi, it makes the right impression except for what Ann considers one "make-or-break detail." Minutes before the camera rolls, she and Lori take black china markers to the wainscoting, drawing a thick black line just beneath the top row of tiles. It's only crayon on trash wood, but the camera sees a fine old tile wall edged in black ceramic.

Two days before filming show thirteen, in which Cookie pedals up to the Codys' wilderness cabin on her bicycle, Jay meets Ann and Ruth on that set. It takes up a corner of the main stage, over where the hotel room and corridor used to be. "What does this look like?" he asks, addressing neither woman in particular. "A city slicker's cabin?" Ruth has created something like a Ralph Lauren fantasy, with camp blankets, horseshoe clothes hooks, and birch-bark picture frames. The kitchen is furnished with a well-worn butcher block and the best of Coleman and Braun (Ruth has saved a bit of money by negotiating product placement with manufacturers; the espresso machine belongs to a crew member). The joke around the set is that John Calvin is undone by kitchen gadgets. "He can't handle a cheese grater," says Jay. "What's he going to do with an espresso machine? Blow up the studio?" The kitchen counter and sink are skirted with a striped madras fabric—cheaper certainly than building cabinets, and the detail is sweet and accurate. "I hope the camera sees that," Ruth says. Chris Cody is obviously someone who knows food and wine; there are ropes of garlic and peppers, the essential cookbooks (Marcella Hazan, Alice Waters), a rack of California cabernets, bottles of good olive oil and balsamic vinegar. And the blue-and-white Bristol ware suits the rustic setting.

Steve favors practical light sources, so Ruth has placed lots of lamps about, including a pair of western-style chimneys from Fantasy Lights, a rental shop that specializes in period, novelty, and fad lighting (it's where you go for pole lamps and lava lamps). Failing to find anything like a cowboy lampshade, Ruth has a couple made, paying a young artist $100 to paint scenes on a couple of paper lampshades.

Through the paneless green-framed windows is wilderness: a painted backdrop of firs and birches supplemented with a fat pine trunk nailed to a stand. Viewed through the fake windows it looks like a tiny, misty green forest, made to match the piney exterior scenes shot just below the famous observatory in Los Angeles's Griffith Park. Jay is pleased with the cabin, which Ann gleefully boasts of as a $28,000 set that she and Mike have created for $17,000. "But it looks even better than twenty-eight grand," she says. "It looks like we poured money into it, and that's exactly what we want. The name of the game is seeing money on the screen." The lumber and dry wall, she points out, are recycled from the hotel corridor set built for two earlier episodes. Through the camera, even the wood-grained linoleum floor looks good, although it's not the wooden planking or faux flagstone she would have preferred. "Jay made a point about the wooden floor, but when Chris and Cookie are down there you really only see them on the rug. Sometimes in television, producers or directors just want sets to look like their own houses."

The cabin is a solid piece of work, with the accent on "solid": "This is real construction," says Ann. "You could stand this in a field and live in it." That may be true of the framing, but the interior details are pure Burbank make-believe. The logs of this log cabin are fiberglass, as are the hearthstones. Craig Nycz, the set painter who works with Mike, is a master of trompe l'oeil, able to make a sheet of paper look like ebony, bronze, marble, or satin. "For *Death Becomes Her* I turned a zero-grade veneer into mahogany," says Craig, whose other credits include the decrepit houses in a horror film by Wes Craven. He works his effects with pantry and toolshed staples: vinegar, salt, coffee, maple syrup, food coloring, oatmeal, cornstarch, fertilizer. For the cabin set in *Smoldering Lust* he does all he can in the three days Ann allots him. "I wish you could pay me for five," he tells her. "Then you'd really have a nice cabin." The days he puts in are long ones: twelve hours or more of standing on ladders, then sitting lotus-legged before the fiberglass fireplace, washing, brushing, rubbing on layer after layer of color and texture. He is always amused to hear that his is either a dying craft or that it's making a come-back. "Trompe l'oeil never went away out here," he says. "The studios can't afford to let it go—faking it saves too much money on materials. What would you rather pay for—split logs or fiber-glass, Siena marble or brown paper?" As Craig works, daubing on color, the featherweight fireplace facade gradually turns to stone. Ruth returns, carrying gingham curtains for the window at the kitchen sink. Looking around, she's clearly pleased. "It's a real log-esque cabin!"

CHAPTER EIGHT
NEXT

MAN: LATE 30S—EARLY 40S, THIS UNFLAPPABLE MECHANIC FROM BUTCH'S TEXACO EMERGES FROM THE WOODS ON FOOT, ARRIVING AT BRODSKY'S BROKEN-DOWN VAN IN RESPONSE TO BRODSKY'S PHONE CALL TO AAA FOR ASSISTANCE. BRODSKY NEARLY BITES HIS HEAD OFF WHEN [HE] ASKS FOR A HAMMER ... I SPEECH & 3 LINES, I SCENE.

STORY LINE: AN UPTIGHT BRODSKY ATTEMPTS AN OUTDOORS WEEKEND IN THE WOODS WITH CODY, BUT THROWS IN THE TOWEL EARLY, AND HEADS BACK TO TOWN IN THE HOPE OF SEDUCING MARGO.

This is how Cheryl Bayer breaks down a nameless character in show eleven, which she is casting just a week before the scene will be shot in Griffith Park. The cameo will give an actor a day's work, $600 in SAG earnings, and most important, exposure—not only to the audience that may tune in but to the makers of *Smoldering Lust,* who may like the actor's work and remember his name for their next show. The few lines of dialogue, the exchange with Brodsky and Cody, are written to be deadpanned. To every actor reading for the part, Cheryl provides "sides," the appropriate pages pulled from the script:

A MAN suddenly emerges out of the woods.

                    CODY
What's this, another customer?

                    BRODSKY
(yelling at the MAN)
Look, we don't have any hammers, okay?

                    MAN
That's not a problem. Open up the hood.

                    BRODSKY
It's road service! What, you don't even bring a truck?

                    MAN
I'm two minutes through the woods if I need anything.

                    BRODSKY
But I was ten miles away from here when I called.

                    MAN
Yeah … and then they call the closest station, which is—
(points to name on shirt)
Butch's Texaco
Brodsky opens the hood and the MAN looks at the engine.
Brodsky and Cody stand nearby [talking between them-
selves while MAN keeps looking under hood].
Cody leaves.

                    BRODSKY
How y'comin'?

                    MAN
Y'got a hammer?
On Brodsky's look,   FADE OUT

The last line is fragile, based on a running joke in the series about Brodsky's van, which is emblazoned with the words ED'S HOUSE OF HAMMERS, and Cheryl needs an actor who can casually throw it off rather than italicize it. The mechanic, she thinks, could be a scene-stealer. "It's one of those little jewels that gets written into a show," she says of the role. "The actor is on and off quickly, but he can make a strong impression. I want to find someone who'll play it cool and calm, like he knows a lot more than he's saying. The mechanic's matter-of-factness is a good counterpart to Brodsky's hot temper."

Her talent searches for such shows as *Fresh Prince of Bel-Air, Herman's Head,* and *Dream On* have earned her a solid reputation, but she hates it that some people call her the queen of comedy casting. "I'm not the queen of anything," she says. "I just do my job. And every season brings a lot of comedies to fill, which excites me." She doesn't mind, however, being known as one of the youngest casting directors in town. "I may be *the* youngest— I'm twenty-seven, not yet twenty-eight."

Nine men are waiting in Cheryl's tiny reception area in her Studio City office this morning, and there's not enough room for all of them to sit down. Some squat on the floor, others lean against the wall; a couple shift nervously from one foot to the other. One of those standing is tall and lean and wears his shirt unbuttoned halfway down his chest, as if he's come to try out for beefcake. Another fellow, stocky, has bleached his hair but too much sun or chlorine or something has oranged it. A heavyweight whose T-shirt just covers his protruding stomach is talking loudly to anyone who will listen about raising longhorn cattle in Colorado. "That's what I'd rather be doing today," he says, "tending the flock." He means herd. Told that he looks like John Goodman, that he could double for him on *Roseanne,* he beams, announcing to the room that he was in fact Goodman's stand-in in *Barton Fink.* "Got hurt doing that film," he says. "Burned my arm in the hotel fire scene." So what's he like? someone wants to know, meaning Goodman. "Who—Johnny? Great, just great." Then, turning his attention to the crowded waiting room: "Think they got enough of us guys in here to read these few lines?"

The chatter seems only to make the men more nervous than they were when they got here. "Not a lot of jobs out there," one offers. There are nods around the room. "Nothing's happening right now," says another actor. "It's too late in the season. Pilots have come and gone." Another: "I hear the situation's better in New York." "Pittsburgh, Vancouver, Toronto, Texas—that's where they're shooting." The wave of commiseration passes, and the unemployed men return to the pages clutched in their hands to run over the lines once again: " … Y'got a hammer?"

Cheryl apologizes to Ron, the first to be called into the spare office she uses for auditions. "I hate to keep people waiting, but that was an important telephone call. Believe me, I'd put off peeing before making someone wait." Ron shrugs. He's not about to complain, especially to Cheryl. In faded jeans and a white oxford-cloth shirt, sharing a sofa with her assistant, Lisa Miller, this casting director strives to put auditioning actors at ease. "I never sit behind a desk when actors come in to read," Cheryl says. "I think it's important to get into the ring with them, to do a good job of reading with them. How can an actor give his all if he's not getting it back from me?"

Raised in New Jersey, Cheryl spent summers in California with an uncle who, she says, "introduced me to the business. He's one of the great people in this town—extremely successful, but also a real human being. He taught me how important it is to treat everyone you work with with decency and kindness, from the star of a show to the guards at the studio." She doesn't offer her uncle's name, but if you prod her she lets on that it's Henry Winkler, the Fonz of TV legend. After college, Cheryl got work as a production assistant on *Happy Days* and on another show produced by Garry Marshall, *Laverne and Shirley.* The move to the casting department of Marshall's company happened easily enough for her. "I kept nagging them and they're the sort of people who go, 'Here's the rope, take how much.' I hope I'm the same way now, encouraging my employees to go for it."

Like most anyone who works in service to actors, including talent agents and personal managers, Cheryl is something of a den mother, always watching out for her clients. Most of them know little about the business side of their profession, as Cheryl discovered when researching her senior thesis in college, "The Other Side of Acting," in which she focused on technicalities that escape the attention of craft-absorbed drama students. "I try to educate them," she says of her brood, "to teach them to be wary." And on a morning like this, spent with "hopefuls" (the term makes actors sound unduly pathetic), she does what she can to minimize the inevitable humiliations of the audition process.

She starts by putting her feet up on the sofa. But friendly as she is, she doesn't suffer lack of preparedness—or talent—and most of this morning's candidates for the mechanic's role, beginning with Ron, are quickly thanked and dismissed. Calling for the next from the holding pen, then the next, and the next, Cheryl and Lisa make quick work of the nine auditions—partly because the scene is so short, less than a minute, but mostly because the actors leave zero doubt that they're not right for the part. *Next.* A stringbean of a figure in a cowboy hat (apparently a misguided attempt to dress in character) blows one of the lines and starts over twice. "Okay, good," Cheryl says sweetly, ending the botched tryout. *Next.* A jolly one bounces in and asks what he should have figured out before he got here: "What's the take on this guy?" His reading is fast and heated. "Too New York Italian," Cheryl says to Lisa after he leaves. *Next.* John Goodman's former stand-in gives a good reading, though Lisa asks him to go again, "real low-key—like you've done this a thousand times, looking under people's hoods." The reading is quieter, more blasé. "Nice adjustment," says Cheryl. "Thank you." Keeping a written record of the process, the women scribble comments, keeping a record of who read what—and how: NO; TOO EAGER; JUST OK; TOO YOUNG; MUMBLES; INTERESTING, NOT FOR THIS SHOW.

The audition is a washout, with no one sent up to read at Empire Studios. Needing a break, Cheryl crosses the street from her office to settle into a booth at Dupar's, a beloved coffee shop chain ("Great food—fine service … southern pecan pie, 1958 Gold Cup Winner"). Though disappointed by the morning's business, she knows her dream mechanic is out there. Turns out his name is Gordon Hurst. An appealing character actor whose on-camera experience dates back to *The Last Picture Show,* Gordon has done lots of television—*The Dukes of Hazzard, The A-Team, Alice.* When his agent, Fred Ansel, left word on Gordon's answering machine ("Hi, this is Gordon! I don't know where I am or what I'm doing right now but I'll call you back … "), something about the message, says the actor, who had just returned from a few days in Big Sur, "felt right." And it was. "I went in, Cheryl was real nice, it was real relaxed. I believed her when she said 'Terrific' at the end."

Shooting in Griffith Park the following week, Gordon just about steals the scene from John and Bradley, raising the hood of the van and then his eyebrows as he says nonchalantly, "Y'got a hammer?"

CHAPTER NINE
SHOPPING

I t's a hot Saturday, July 4. Despite the holiday, all the stores are open in Beverly Hills, and Lani Reynolds is working them, shopping for Margo. "She's going to need something to snuggle into next week," says petite, redheaded Lani, turning over her Mazda Protege to the parking valet behind I. Magnin on Wilshire. "Margo's feeling vulnerable right now, after her roll with Brodsky on the bedroom floor. She's scared. She was naughty, and she knows it. So I'm going to wrap her in a bulky turtleneck or cardigan. Off-white, maybe, to convey her virtue— she and Brodsky did stop themselves, after all."

Entering the store, Lani allows herself one moment of distraction, at a perfume counter ("Whiffs of lavender from the south of France, that's all the vacation I get this summer," she sighs), before proceeding to the elevator and up to Magnin's studio services department on the fourth floor. Here, counseled by smart young women, Lani and other designers assemble wardrobes for television characters. Viktoria Kaye, the recent Parsons graduate who runs the department, already knows about Margo Cody, and when something arrives in the store that seems right for the character, she sets it aside for Lani.

Viktoria is a personal shopper for make-believe people. Her domain at Magnin is a beige alcove adjacent to the couture salons. Posters along one wall (JANE SEYMOUR IN *SUN STROKE)* form a sort of visual résumé for the department. There are comfortable chairs, telephones at the ready. "Coffee, Lani?" Viktoria asks. "Bottled water?" The water is served in wine glasses.

The Magnin studio department is not unique. Stores all over town offer the service, catering to television producers keeping a hard eye on costs. Rather than hire costume designers to create and care for originals, most productions either rent clothes from costume houses, or buy from such blue-chip department stores as this one, or Saks, or Neiman-Marcus. A few independent retailers may also do business with the production companies, smart shops such as Fred Segal on Melrose or Mr. Frank in Santa Monica. The usual deal is this: you check out as many garments as you like to try out on the actors and run by whoever else may need to be consulted—directors, producers. Directors of photography and lighting engineers may wish to comment on colors and patterns. The clothes may be kept for five days. After that, return what you don't want, and pay for what you keep—at full retail price. Since her first job in television—stitching up the Lennon Sisters' pastel gowns on *The Lawrence Welk Show* in 1982, its last year of production—Lani has designed clothes for many sitcoms and hour-long dramas, but not for *Smoldering Lust*. "This isn't about sketching and stitching, really," she says. "It's about shopping. I'm filling closets for the characters."

"You just missed Donna Mills," Viktoria says. "She was here for her new movie-of-the-week. It's about a journalist who's had a baby with a political candidate whose campaign she's covering. Very smart wardrobe." Indicating a small mountain of dresses and jackets, she adds, "That's just the first selection." Lani can hardly bear to look. "Must be nice to have some money to spend," she says. "I'm saddled with a budget that must have been put together by an idiot, someone who obviously hasn't bought anything off the rack since the seventies." At $2,000 an episode, the budget is indeed puny, especially for a show with eight regular characters. It seems an unwise place to economize; the milieu, after all, is fashion. The Cody Canyon look, modeled on something like Ralph Lauren's Polo line, doesn't come cheap.

"We're shooting shows four, five, and six next week," Lani tells Viktoria, who has already set aside a few things for consideration. "The wardrobe's basically set. I'm just filling in today, and looking ahead a bit. How'd we do on Margo's sweater look?" Viktoria shows her something in gray cashmere, a sweatshirt by Calvin Klein. "A cocoon," says Viktoria. "Something Margo can hide in by the fire." Lani likes it, not just because it's right for the scene but because it can be worn again, too—thrown around the shoulders, tied around the waist. Margo Cody may be a fashion-conscious woman, but her wardrobe is nothing like Murphy Brown's. In her thirteen-episode life, Margo will wear the same cocktail dress three times.

Though Lani has opted for the glorified sweatshirt, she likes to have other possibilities to show Kate, so she makes a fast tour of departments on two floors—scanning, swooping in, sizing up. Clothes hangers screech right to left, left to right on the shining steel racks. "This," she says, pulling out something in bright yellow, "is lovely." It's a day dress by Anna Sui, cut well above the knee and with broad shoulder straps; the leggy Kate could kill in it. But at $375, it's too expensive. Returning to the studio services lounge, Lani signs for the $90 sweatshirt.

When starting work on a new show, Lani reads as many scripts as she can, breaking them down for wardrobe purposes. Little is specified about costumes in the scripts for *Smoldering Lust,* however, and it is through casual meetings with Jay that she begins to envision how the characters should look. They agree that Margo's assistant Philip is natty, showing never a wrinkle and that Eve likes her clothes two ways—tight and revealing. Brodsky is a thrift-shop hound. "He dresses sort of like I do," says Jay, who is fond of loose shirts and beat-up shoes, and he suggests to Lani that Brodsky wear the same old pair of jeans most of the time.

"You can dress him at the Salvation Army," he tells her, and she does.

"How about Hawaiian shirts?" Lani asks.

"Good. And a baseball jacket—but not necessarily his. Some school he's never heard of." The search for Brodsky's uniform will take Lani to secondhand shops all over Hollywood—well-known spots such as the American Rag Company, plus an obscure *Wunderkammer* or two whose names she will not reveal.

On the rare occasions when Brodsky wears a suit, it's a costume-house rental. "No need to buy him one," Jay says. "Brodsky wouldn't buy himself one, not a new suit anyway." *Smoldering Lust* isn't the only production that resorts to rentals. "It's not ideal," says Lani, "and you feel sort of compromised, like one in a crowd, but it's become necessary."

Lani sorts purchases in her office at Empire, which she shares with her assistant, Lisa Wilson, and Brenda Maben. As set costumer, Brenda is responsible for what she calls "clothing continuity." Slipping on and off the set with a Polaroid, Brenda snaps actors immediately before and after each take, to ensure the consistency of their appearance. For Bradley Whitford, that might mean making sure that the sleeves of his rumpled shirt are rolled up to just below the elbow one day, and that the left, not the right, shoelace is untied.

The few references to wardrobe in the script are small jokes about things like Eve's getups for her Cody Canyon modeling sessions, Brodsky's disguises, and Felton's loud boxer shorts. Lani can punch up a joke with her costume choices, as she does when she puts Chris in little-boy cowboy pajamas and Margo in a dominatrix-style nightie that she meekly describes as being "illegal in the Midwest." The show has a running visual gag having to do with Toads, Hal Kemper's "amphibious athletic shoes." What Hal claims is the "official shoe of northern California" should look ridiculous, Jay tells Lani, "not unlike a propeller beanie."

Joining in the lead discussion is David Glazer, prop master. The project falls not entirely within wardrobe's realm nor the prop department's, and David enjoys the chance to collaborate with Lani. "If she can give me the basic shoe you want," he tells Jay, "I'll do whatever extra to it. What about eyes—do Toads have eyes?" Lani has already wondered that herself. She takes from her pocket the two halves of a bisected Ping-Pong ball. "In my fantasies," she says, "I see these somehow bulging out with every step Hal takes." Notes for the outline of show two mention a built-in hydraulic system for the shoe. David says he could attach a squeeze pump to the heel, "something like on a perfume atomizer." But after fiddling with a mock-up he abandons the idea. "This could be a nightmare. We'll be doing extra takes because it'll keep falling off. And I'm not so sure the camera would even see the pump." Lani and David agree that the shoe should be painted a high-gloss green, and that in the end is all it turns out to be: garishly green. The discussion about other flourishes for the Toads—fins, flippers, a vile red tongue—loses steam. The lacquered green shoes may not be the funniest sight gag ever, but they do meet Jay's requirement of looking absurd, especially when worn by a grown man.

In episode four, Hal sets fire to the Toads to prove their indestructibility. The demonstration takes place in the Cody Canyon offices, atop Philip's desk, where the shoes blaze in the background while Hal makes his sales pitch. The nonsense lasts only a minute on-screen, but Lani must make elaborate preparations before hand with a special effects technician. Arriving on the set early one morning, Howard Jensen announces that he is about to "show you ladies exactly what can be done with certain flammable liquids." He is speaking to Lani and director Lesli Glatter. With thirty-odd years of experience in the business, Howard calls himself an "all-purpose special effects man. I do fire, snow, rain. Any kind of weather. I rig cars. God, I used to love to do explosions." Compared to making a Model-T flip over, as he did for *Bonnie and Clyde,* or inverting and flooding the staterooms of an ocean liner, as he did for *Beyond the Poseidon Adventure,* the pyrotechnical stunt is a snap. But that doesn't make Howard slacken. "Beware the routine jobs," he says. "That's when things backfire. I always worry about the little things. Just when you relax—boom." Looking on is a Burbank fire marshal, whose official presence is mandatory on any set that employs fire, even in rehearsal. Howard unpacks a cardboard box containing Zippo lighter fluid, rubber cement, charcoal fuel, a wand igniter. At least ten crew members gather for the test, including David (in case there are problems with props), Ann Champion (to deal with anything relevant to set design), and Steve Confer (who needs to decide how the camera will photograph the flames). Just before Howard douses the Toads, Lani cracks: "Can we afford this test? Which department's going to spring for the new shoes?"

Lesli doesn't like the Zippo fire. "I want a *whoosh* when it's lit," she says. "Bigger flames, lots of smoke." Steve nixes the smoke, which would cloud the camera. Howard points out that the rubber cement, since it is brushed, not poured, onto the shoes, localizes the flames. "It gives a nice, slow burn, more blue than orange." By combining it with a little charcoal lighter, which ignites in tall flames of orange and yellow, he produces exactly the effect Lesli and Lani want. Turning to the fire marshal, Lani asks if she'll have to fireproof the costumes. She won't, he replies, as long as he's standing by with a fire extinguisher. Ruth Bracken asks the same about the set furnishings; she'll have to remove one of the rugs hanging on the wall. Packing up, Howard has a few more words for Lesli and Lani. "Make sure your actors are cool about this. I've had people freak out on me with their fears. Like Buddy Hackett. He panicked in *Love Bug,* when we turned him upside down in the Volkswagen. The blubber fell down around his face and he thought he was going to suffocate. So just make sure your actors are okay about fire."

❧ ❧ ❧

"How's that Donna Karan jacket working out?" asks Bobbe Aiona, head of studio services at Saks Fifth Avenue. It's mid-August and Lani is shopping once again for Margo. "The red is gorgeous," Lani says. "Kate's already worn it twice, and I need you to start looking around for something to combine it with. Maybe a little shell dress. Navy, probably, and sleeveless—we'll be shooting in a car, outside, and it could get pretty uncomfortable." The evidence that Bobbe has been in this business awhile is on the wall, which is hung with eight-by-ten glossies, each autographed and bearing a star's thanks and kisses: Barbara Eden, Elizabeth Montgomery, Linda Gray, Loni Anderson. "Still smoldering?" Bobbe asks Lani, echoing the amusement around town about the show's title.

"Absolutely," says Lani. "We're all set to go on the next three shows. I'm thinking ahead today. I want a different sort of look for Margo's next big night with Brodsky. I'm thinking about a riding outfit. Not jodhpurs, exactly, but something tight and tapered. Boots, a short black jacket." Bobbe points her toward the Ralph Lauren collection, and Lani spots what she's thinking of: jodhpurs without the exaggerated thighs, stretch cotton, tan, $175. She also grabs a pair of black leggings and a white crew-neck sweater and signs for them on the production's loan sheet.

Heading out of Saks, Lani passes a series of couture salons—Valentino, Versace, Chanel—and holds a hand up, shielding her eyes. "I don't dare look," she says. "Can't afford to." A Vicky Tiel cocktail dress is the show's single luxury item. At $1,400, it threatened to consume nearly all of one episode's wardrobe budget when Lani found it shortly before production began. Swirling the dress before Elaine Arata and Harriette Ames-Regan, the unit production manager, she made her pitch: "I like it, and Kate adores it. She feels comfortable in it and it's perfect for the ballroom." Her two-woman audience was frowning, but Lani had a clincher: "Don't forget, this is the first time audiences will see

Kate. This is her entrance. Her TV debut, in fact. It's got to be stunning." Besides, there was hardly any time left for more shopping; the day after she'd been cast, Kate accompanied Lani on a shopping trip to find Margo's dress. The schedule seemed impossible: they discovered the dress on a Thursday, with shooting to begin the following Tuesday. It was now Friday. So Lani got what she and Kate wanted, but only after promising that Kate would wear the dress at least two more times, so that the cost could be spread out over other episodes. Consulting the writers, Lani found that a second ballroom scene is planned, and she figured she could tone down the Tiel gown for a restaurant scene Rick was working on. Amortized in this way, the costume was affordable, but just. "I'll go easy on the accessories," Lani promised, thinking of a ten-dollar string of pearls she'd spotted at Nordstrom's.

As production continues, Lani's office fills with clothes—piles, boxes, racks of them. Hats, shoes, scarves, and handbags are spilling off shelves. Alterations are a constant part of the activity here, and the three women who inhabit the office are never without needle and thread. Beyond the ironing boards and sewing machine table, Lani's head is just visible over a stack of hatboxes. A souvenir mug from *Who's the Boss* sits on her desk. "Now *that* show had a budget," she says.

Echo Park is not the prosperous enclave of Los Angeles it once was, no longer considered safe, but for a few August nights, one of its hilltop houses makes the neighborhood shine again as the Codys' handsome San Francisco residence. Past midnight, Kate and Alison still have a few hours left of filming a front-porch scene. Lani has arranged to talk to Kate in the hair and makeup trailer, one of a dozen oversized vehicles parked along the closed-off streets, about her wardrobe for the final episode of the series. Kate won't be able to go shopping with Lani next week; once this scene wraps, she's off to Hawaii to watch the filming of *Jurassic Park*. Alison, perched in the next chair, runs her lines with a visitor to the location shoot while Lani and Kate try to figure out what to do for the final episode, which involves a flashback. "It's nineteen-seventy-something," Lani tells Kate. "Margo's a kid."

"Margo's totally in love with Cody, right?" the actress replies.

"Smitten. So what do we do to get you back to that time? Your hair will be in a braid. A dress? Jeans?"

"Jeans! Faded jeans! And sneakers."

"Jeans with Weejuns. Don't forget, it's the seventies."

"I love jeans with Weejuns!" Kate exclaims. "*I* wore jeans with Weejuns!"

Soon they've got the look figured out: old Levi's with white socks and Weejuns, a plaid flannel shirt. No belt. Hair and makeup will take care of the rest.

In the vast, dimly lit lobby of the Park Plaza Hotel, a spooky, vaguely Egyptian-style landmark on MacArthur Park near downtown Los Angeles, it looks as though a major motion picture is in the making (as many have been, beginning in 1927 with Cecil B. DeMille's *My Friend from India)*. Scores of people are strolling about, most of them in black evening clothes. There are sequins and ostrich boas, shiny bugle beads, skirts of chiffon and satin. Some among the crowd carry champagne flutes and highball glasses, though the drinks are soft. It's not yet nine in the morning.

Working with extras on location, Lani becomes a drill sergeant, and her orders are specific. She has insisted that the men bring black tie; no facsimiles will be allowed. White dinner jackets, like the one Chris wears in the scene, are fine. "But not too many," she told them. The women have been instructed to arrive with at least two dark evening dresses. Lani envisions a room full of muted colors. "The mood of the scene is ominous. There's a dead girl upstairs. We don't want it looking too frivolous down here in the ballroom." The extras all nodded when Lani reminded them that they were supposed to be in "elegant, conservative" San

Francisco, at a formal occasion, a political fund-raiser, but some still don't make the cut and are sent home, like schoolchildren who have violated a dress code. "I hate turning anyone away," says Lani. "People need work. But when it's hopeless, what do you do?" One woman sports a brown sheath. "Give me a choice," Lani tells her. "What else did you bring?" This is it, the woman says, and she's out. A young man has improvised his ensemble from the dregs of his closet: black jeans; a black linen jacket, stained and snug; a regular white shirt, its collar folded and ironed into a makeshift wing collar. "Excuse me," says Lani, amused, "but who exactly do you think you're fooling?" Taking pity, she scares up a spare dinner jacket and a pair of black trousers that just about fit. "I'll work with almost anyone," she says. "As long as there's some hope, and as long as no one sasses me. I'll try to make most anything work."

For the most part the men are fine, even if some of the tuxedos are a little threadbare. Such details get lost in the crowd. "But the women!" Lani cries. "Especially the white gals, cramming their size-forty-four selves into thirty-eights. And so many of them have that horrible teased hair. The ones who think they're so adorable at fifty, they're the ones you have to watch out for. Why can't they learn from the black and Asian women here—they're divine."

One of the best dressed is Al Verdun, who produces a business card from her satin evening bag. Stamped with a tiny portrait of herself, the card lists her trades and talents: ACTRESS•SINGER•WRITER•MODEL. Al has lost count, but figures this must be at least her twentieth walk-on of the year. It's better than the others, though; she won't just be sitting there this time, fake-talking, fake-laughing, fake-drinking: "I get to do some crossing," she says, thrilled. Crossing: for an extra, walking past the front of the camera represents a break, a tiny step up. Some blow the chance by seizing the moment a little too aggressively, upstaging the speaking actors—as one extra did to Bradley during the closing monologue of the eighth episode, making a fuss with her purse and staring into the camera as if into an aquarium. (Incredibly enough, no one caught her in the act, and Leslie Dennis, in the film-editing bay, couldn't rescue the scene, which had to be reshot at Empire on a hastily built and decorated set.)

Al Verdun isn't about to trip up like that. She is smart and patient, and seemingly as optimistic as an aspiring actor-singer-writer-model can get. "Now all I need are some good speaking lines. Whoever discovers me will make lots of money. You know what my favorite song is? The one that goes 'open up the door and I'll shut it myself.' James Brown sings it and that's what I'm saying. Just give me a chance." With that, she twirls and dances a few steps, a livelier figure than most in the lobby of the Park Plaza Hotel on a groggy Thursday morning. "Maybe I'm halfway there. The wardrobe lady told me that my dress was perfect for the scene."

Over the summer Lani amasses hundreds of garments and accessories, about $30,000 worth of clothes. She must make a detailed inventory, then arrange storage of it. A major studio, looking everywhere for revenues today, would likely add the wardrobe to its own massive inventory and rent items out to productions around town. The system was once more generous, with producers inviting actors to help themselves to whatever costumes they fancied. Crew members could then pick through the leftovers. Until NBC decides the future of *Smoldering Lust*, Brillstein-Grey must foot the bill for wardrobe storage. If the show is killed, Lani hopes the company will give the actors first crack at their wardrobes. The rest could then be sold to a costume house or consigned to A Star is Born, a Hollywood outlet that sells recycled film and television wardrobes. In these tightfisted days, a producer's 50 percent share of a thrift shop's take on a few boxes of old clothes dare not be discounted.

CHAPTER TEN
BEAT IT OUT, 2

The Writers Guild requires television producers to hire out at least two of every thirteen episodes to freelancers. The producers of *Smoldering Lust* don't object to the rule, although their fear is pretty much borne out: that Jay and Rick and Russ do seem to be the only people on earth who can write this particular show. Before shooting has begun, a call for script submissions goes out in the *Hollywood Reporter,* and the task of sorting through all the material that comes back and fielding telephone calls from writers' agents falls to Rick. "You really want to give people a crack," he says, "but the scripts I'm seeing are written too broadly. We can't do this show with sitcom writers. We need screenwriters and playwrights." Rick has only to look back home to New York to find theater colleagues eager to give the show a try: "God knows they need the money," says Rick, himself having graduated from off-Broadway to network TV pay. But the two he hires have enormous difficulty producing the 25-30 pages that make up an average half-hour television script. Even with scripts and several filmed episodes to study, the playwrights somehow can't get the tone of *Smoldering Lust* down. Rick gives them copious notes, waits for rewrites, sends more notes. Finally he rewrites himself. "It doesn't mean they're not good writers," he says, "just not the right match for the material. You either have an ear cocked for this kind of stuff or you don't."

Precious weeks are consumed on the back-and-forth with freelancers, and toward the end of the summer production threatens to come to a standstill. Without scripts, nothing can happen down the line: Liz doesn't know what locations to scout, Lani can't shop for wardrobe, Ann can't design new sets, Ruth has no rooms to decorate. Ultimately it is the original team of Jay, Rick, and Russ who write all thirteen scripts, although the show credits don't read that way. As Russ says, "You had to be there at the beginning, when we laid all this out for the first time." And so the original three continue to beating it out.

JAY: "Cookie's jealous of Margo, resents her. Margo has everything. Let's put something in about that. 'Women like her make it hard for women like me …'"

RICK: "What does Cookie know? What does she hear?"

RUSS: "It's an airtight plot line when you read it, everything's going along like it should, but now it seems there's some looseness to it. Can we write over it, keep the plot but just find out where everybody is emotionally?"

JAY: "The last time we saw Cody he was in bed with Margo, so we're going to have to set up a lot of stuff in Brodsky's narration. We've got a lot happening off camera in this show."

RICK: "Well, the only thing that's really happened off camera is Cody and Eve's agreement to meet in the motel."

JAY: "Yeah, but that's after he and Margo had great sex at the end of show four. What's wrong with this guy? Wasn't that enough? I don't trust the motel setup. We have to make sure we know he's there only to tell Eve that he's breaking off their affair."

RUSS: "The affair that never happened."

JAY: "Right, the non-affair. 'Eve, we can't go on *not* going on like this.' We've got to see Eve at the motel, leaving Cody there. That'll help her image, too.

"Meanwhile, what about Margo and Brodsky? Margo has just told Brodsky that she doesn't need him anymore, that she's gonna stay in her marriage: 'I'm going to make this thing work. You're fired.' So Brodsky, to stay in the picture, has to convince Margo that her husband's a vicious killer. Why? Because he wants to be with Margo? Is that normal—is that a *semi*-normal motivation?"

RUSS: "Sounds good to me. Margo has the hots for her husband, whether he's a murderer or not. She's telling Brodsky to back off."

RICK: "And Brodsky's going, 'God, I'm in love with her and now she's fucking this guy and she may even love him more now that he's a killer. So maybe the only thing I can do is get him convicted so I can have her to myself.' "

JAY: "But she's still attracted to Brodsky in some ways. I mean, she doesn't *not* have the hots for Brodsky."

RICK: "Right. In the record store she's still pulling him against herself like she did before. Very close."

JAY: "The way I'm starting to look at Brodsky is that he's actually a parody of a Sam Spade kind of cop, one of those hard-boiled guys who look like that and act like that. There's a little bit of that about him, but it's all, like, this facade."

RICK: "I like that."

JAY: "And he can't believe it that things work out in that cli‐chéd way. Like, he finds a note in Cody's breast pocket, and it's a comment on all those stereotyped ways that detectives find clues. It really happens that way and Brodsky's just amazed. Every detective cliché proves to be one hundred percent accurate as he goes along."

RUSS: "But he just can't figure out why he doesn't smoke, because all detectives smoke—"

RICK: "I was going to ask if he smokes."

JAY: "I don't know. If he does he doesn't inhale. It's for effect. Maybe he wears a hat—don't detectives wear hats?"

RUSS: "Clues just fall into his lap. Like, someone says, 'I had nothing to do with that bludgeoning death.' Then: 'Who said anything about a bludgeon?' It's all absurdly neat."

JAY: "And if it's far-fetched, I think you should comment on it. Any cliché we do should be commented on. That's why they're clichés—because they happen."

In the beginning Brodsky may come across as Sam Spade, as the writers intend him to be, but as the series unfolds he turns out to be more like Barney Fife, an arrogant know-it-all, unable to smell evidence under his nose and burdened with an exaggerated sense of his attractiveness to women. Russ seems to understand Brodsky's true jerky nature, underscoring it in an ongoing bit about the detective's surveillance van, which has the words ED'S HOUSE OF HAMMERS painted across it.

RUSS: "While Brodsky's sitting outside the motel in the van, he gets a parking ticket for parking in a loading zone or something. Or maybe someone wants to buy a hammer."

JAY: "Oh, right, it's Ed's House of Hammers."

RUSS: "Or some kids are taking the wheels off the back of the van and he gets out and says, 'What the hell are you doing?' "

JAY: "I like that about somebody trying to buy a hammer. Gets real pissed off when Brodsky doesn't have one. He could use an excuse like 'I don't have any on me, they're all in the store.' "

RUSS: " 'You have to special-order them.' "

JAY: " 'The store is downtown.'—'I need a hammer now.'—'I don't have hammers.'—'What *have* you got?'—'Everything else.' "

RUSS: " 'You don't have hammers? How can you call yourself a House of Hammers? Could I please have a hammer?' "

JAY: "I think it'd be funny if a guy just kept insisting that he needed a hammer."

RUSS: "Then he says, 'I want to talk to Ed. Are you Ed?' "

JAY: " 'I've got to talk to Ed. I'm sure I'm not the only guy who needs a hammer today. Mine broke, I need a new one.' "

RUSS: " 'Here, here—go buy a hammer. There's a hardware store two blocks away.'—'Oh, I don't know—I had my heart set on one of Ed's hammers ... ' I like the idea of a page and a half or so of hammer stuff."

JAY: "Let's do it."

Brodsky would of course like to believe that Chris Cody is the killer so that he can pursue Margo. But Chris does finally convince him of his innocence, in a scene hatched over a writers' lunch on May Day:

JAY: "I don't think Brodsky thinks Cody's the killer until he goes into the motel room, do you? But it's okay if he pretends to think so, so he can get to Margo. But he must know that Cody couldn't kill anybody."

RUSS: "So he goes into the motel room and Brodsky alludes to Cody as a suspect. But Cody says, 'I couldn't be a killer, I just couldn't do it.' Then, 'Come here.'—Jay, how sleazy is this motel? Can we get a coffeepot set up in the motel room, a sugar bowl?"

JAY: "Well, you can't get room service in this dump, so yeah, we can have a coffeepot. But no other amenities! It's off the beaten path; that's why Eve chose it, to protect Cody. And there's something exciting about an almost-sleazy room."

RUSS: "As long as there's a coffeepot. Not even a kitchenette, a hot plate will do. So Cody shows Brodsky this trail of ants and says, 'Twenty minutes ago this scout ant was in here and I couldn't kill it. I knew there were gonna be more ants coming, and I should've killed it. But I broke down when I looked into its eyes ... '—Do you think that works?"

JAY: "I love the logic of it: he couldn't kill the ant, he must be innocent."

The "ant scene," as it comes to be known, at first seems to require the services of an "insect wrangler," one of the more fantastic job titles in Burbank and Hollywood, but David Glazer in the props department suggests the more economical measure of bringing ants from home. His ants do just as they're supposed to, which is to follow a line of sugar from a coffeepot to the table's edge, past Chris's sympathetic gaze.

"What else about the motel?" Jay asks Russ. "What about health problems? Safe sex—have we done anything with that? Should we do it here?"

Russ writes a last-minute scene for Chris and Eve that necessitates a morning run to the Pleasure Chest, a Hollywood sex shop, by Evan Klein, David's assistant. He returns to the studio with about a dozen condoms. The scene is mildly funny, with Chris, sitting with Eve on the bed (both fully clothed, he in a bright yellow duster), contemplating a condom dangling from his hand like an empty balloon. Why is it unrolled? Doesn't he even know how to use it? The focus on the character's ineptness may be appropriate, but it also thwarts the erotic charge Jay asks Russ to create for the scene, telling him to "make it as hot as you can make it in there. Make it really hard for Cody to get out of this one." Balking again, Chris turns a seduction into a lecture on the technological marvel of latex.

A lunchtime chat between Russ and Jay leads to a funny bit in show twelve between the Waspy Chris and the Jewish Brodsky.

JAY: "Is there anything about Brodsky being Jewish? I think there's a sort of classic fascination there. Brodsky could say, 'You're anti-Semitic.' Then Margo says, 'What do you mean by that?' Brodsky says, 'You don't know what "anti-Semitic" means?' "

RUSS: "We could have Brodsky and Cody talking about famous Jewish detectives. A very short list. Cody finally says, 'You're a Jew, aren't you? I don't know many Jews. What's this about Jews can't name their male babies Junior?' "

Finally Brodsky confides in Chris, telling him that he's had a hard time in life. Because he doesn't look Jewish (as Bradley indeed does not), Jews don't like him, but because he really is Jewish, Gentiles don't like him either. Chris offers that he too has had a hard time as a tall, blond, handsome Wasp. "You're always expected to know how to run things and be in control," he says. "This is no bed of roses."

How boldly, Rick wonders, can Brodsky break the fourth wall in speaking directly to the audience? For episode seven he's been toying with the idea of going over the edge in exposing the artifice. "When Brodsky's in the hotel corridor doing his closing narration," he says, "we could have him knock on Felton and Towanda's door and say, 'Can you keep it down in there? I'm trying to talk into this microphone.' Then she could say, 'Just get that camera and those lights out of here!' She's really mad."

JAY: "And maybe there's a shot of Brodsky walking down the hall with the crew. Is that a good idea, or is it too much? Will it kill the suspense?"
RUSS: "I don't know; it could be funny."
JAY: "Just have a camera crew follow him ... I don't know."
RUSS: "She says, 'Go on, all of you—get!' "

They like the idea of shattering the fourth wall completely, but realize it would cause the network suits to come running. Brodsky's addresses to viewers remain conventional—but less like Bruce Willis's in *Moonlighting,* Jay hopes, than Humphrey Bogart as Sam Spade.

Watching dailies, learning what each actor can do, the writers begin to add layers to the characters. Maggie Han is a revelation, and her role as Cookie evolves from a mousy wallflower to an assertive, intelligent woman. Hiding behind Clark Kent eyeglasses and baggy overalls for the first few episodes, Cookie essentially takes over Brodsky's business and begins to assert her various desires. Maggie, so quick with a line that she becomes a favorite of the writers, shares a practical-to-a-fault streak with the character she plays—the result, she says, of riding the unexpected turns her life has taken. A year after graduating from Harvard, she was strutting down Madison Avenue as the Leggs girl. She doesn't miss the life of a New York model. "This is a lot more fun than modeling panty hose," she says of playing Cookie.

Jay: "Brodsky knows his gut reactions are always one hundred percent wrong, but he goes by them anyway. Whenever he decides not to take a case, Cookie could go, 'Great—another sound business decision.' She's really bright. For lack of a better comparison, she reminds me of Carla on *Cheers*—not that I can look at her—and she reminds me a little of Susan Dey on *L.A. Law*."

Russ: "Right. Someone who says, 'Well, that's bullshit.' "

Jay: "Everything Brodsky says *is* bullshit, but everything she says is bullshit too—like her conspiracy theories. And why does she always think like that? Because of her own life, which is totally screwed up. She may be able to cut through Brodsky, but she can't cut through herself. We shouldn't have to analyze her, just have her be this way because it's fun."

Russ: "There's such conviction in her anger. Her complexity is all there."

Jay: "Here's a woman who doesn't make a lot of money, and she has this kid she supports. She could probably get a better job—"

Russ: "She could go to work for the Department of Motor Vehicles, but this is more interesting, being the girl Friday of a private detective. And it lets her have a field day with her conspiracy theories—even if she is bitter about the money. And she's sort of in love with her boss. In the antagonistic sense."

Jay: "But she'd never let on. She'd never send him flowers. Or she'd bring him flowers but not put them in water: 'Here, these are for you. But don't get the wrong impression. Don't think I like you. These are because I hate you. I'm doing this for me, not for you. I've been acting badly and I just don't like myself.' "

RUSS: " 'I really don't care what they do for you but they make me feel better about myself.' "

JAY: " 'If you want to put them in water, fine.' "

RUSS: " 'I don't know what to say, a woman giving me flowers.' "

JAY: " 'Do whatever you feel like doing with these things.'—Whoa—this is going to get way out of hand if we keep going."

RUSS: "We'll have a sixty-page script."

A lengthy note on the script for show eleven reveals the writer's belated response to the network's equally belated opinion of the scripts. "Basically I think it's great," Jay writes Russ about his script for the episode. "It's exactly what NBC wants ... [But the] characters of Cody and Eve are getting repetitive. We need to find new avenues for them. Cody needs to get more concerned ... rather than always be a total dilettante.

"Many funny scenes ... Margo and Cody in studio at end could be dynamite but it seems to drift away."

The word from NBC is the first writers have heard for nearly two months, when Warren Littlefield called Rick and Jay into his office to tell them how excited he was about the series, how he was going to put promotional muscle behind it. ("You didn't actually believe any of that, did you?" Jay asked Rick afterwards.) But no news since from the network does not, alas, mean good news. Warren and Kevin Reilly are worried about the fact that the writers are doing what they promised they would not do—that is, drag out the murder case. Kevin's concern is that the characters and situations—entire episodes, really—are going nowhere. "The cast, the photography, individual lines are fine," he says. "There's very funny scene work, and I love the premise and the tone. But I feel like I'm reading the same episode over and over again. The dynamics of the relationships aren't growing week to week. It's frustrating. I want to say to Margo, 'All right, so sleep with Brodsky already! *Do* something!' You could drop in anywhere in this series—take all the episodes so far, scramble them up, and you couldn't tell which one is number three or which is nine. I've sent scripts around the office with a note attached, asking, 'Am I crazy or what?' But the consensus is that it's deeply confusing and frustrating. Nobody in the show ever does anything!"

Unashamed to admit that he had no idea what the hell was going on in the scripts, Kevin finally asked, more than halfway into the summer, for a scene that would reintroduce the main characters and get the story back on track. The writers obligingly returned to the ballroom setting of the first episode, where the major players would again appear and their actions and interests perhaps be clarified.

JAY: "This is perfect for what NBC's problem is. We can have people coming through the door of the ballroom and they could almost freeze while Brodsky explains who they are, why they're there. As a way of getting us back to where we should be."

RUSS: "And I don't think we need four pages to do it."

JAY: "Not at all. And maybe Brodsky could be wearing something ridiculous, like a mariachi costume—"

RUSS: "He's working undercover anyway. *Why* is he working undercover?"

RICK: "He wasn't invited."

RUSS: "He wants to see Margo—in show six he leaves her in the bedroom. We need to say why Brodsky is there in the ballroom. That's vague now."

JAY: "Some of that undercover stuff doesn't make sense to me. He's watching somebody, right? So it seems to me that we have to know why he's there. He's undercover, but I don't know why. I've just lost that."

RICK: "Given the way the last show ends, where Brodsky goes to Felton's room and Towanda denies knowing Felton, then—"

RUSS: "Felton's now his primary suspect."

RICK: "Then this gala is how he gets to Felton?"

JAY: "Hence the disguise. But what if people think that maybe he just likes to dress up?"

RUSS: "Let's state it very specifically. This is a golden opportunity to see everybody involved in one place."

RICK: "Should Brodsky be working as a waiter, too?"

JAY: "I like that, serving hors d'oeuvres. And let's play him a little angry that everyone knows who he is. Because he's watching somebody."

RICK: "He's watching Felton."

JAY: "Oh, yeah."

RICK: "And everyone recognizes him."

JAY: "What about Margo?"

RICK: "I think she should still lust after him, but not so openly. Should she punish him?"

JAY: "Her attitude should be, 'What the hell are you doing here?' She could tell him how ridiculous he looks in a mariachi suit."

RICK: "We do leave her in a pretty humiliating place in that scene in six, and I think we need to explain more. Her attitude has got to be pissed off at him."

RUSS: "Which'll probably turn him on."

JAY: "Eating the husk of the tamale is great. Somebody really did that, didn't they?"

RICK: "Gerald Ford."

JAY: "So this guy eats a tamale and is rescued by Brodsky. The only problem I have is this, and it's just a question: Is Cody once again just too inept? He can't even help a guy who's choking on tamales?"

Well, so much for getting the series back on track. If the development folks over at NBC had overheard this beat-out session, they might have groaned in unison. Riding their riffs, the writers apparently had already forgotten what it was exactly that the network asked of them.

CHAPTER ELEVEN
SYNTHESIZER, SAX, AND SUE

Concentrating on the heinous crime that's complicating his life, Brodsky tells his assistant, Cookie, how she can help. "Make yourself useful," he says. "Put on some music." She does.

> BRODSKY
> What the hell is that?

> COOKIE
> Accordion Cavalcade.

> BRODSKY
> Are you crazy?

> COOKIE
> You said to put on some music.

> BRODSKY
> That's not music. I need jazz. Gotta think.

Jazz lazes all through *Smoldering Lust,* deepening the moodiness of the show and intensifying the characters' introspection. Jay pretty much had a score in his head when he first began writing the series. Marginal notes in the outline for the premiere episode call for "tenor saxophone music … softly playing from an

FM radio somewhere." The music sets the tone for the series. It's easy to believe that Dave Brodsky, a man who carries jazz tunes around in his head, would gladly give up the Cody case and the rest of his lame detective work and focus on his record store alone, if he could make a living from it. If Margo has a rival for Brodsky's affections, it's a hi-fi playing in the corner of the shop. Watching Jay work on the show's score with composer Patrick Williams, you get the idea that he too would just as soon swap places with the owner of some musty LP emporium. For weeks he's been praising *Haunted Heart,* new from the Charlie Haden Quartet. "It's a great album," he says, meaning CD, and indeed it is, with new mixes of classic vocals by Jo Stafford, Billie Holiday, and Jeri Southern. Music is important to *Smoldering Lust,* and not just in terms of scoring: almost every script contains a subtle jazz reference or a nod to a popular song, such as Margo's muttering to herself in show ten about being "starry-eyed and vaguely discontented." Lifted from Rodgers and Hammerstein's "It Might as Well Be Spring," the line is buried in the text, like a "Nina" hidden in an Al Hirschfeld caricature. Most other references to musical subjects are less subtle, such as a gag about accordions, a slight variation on a routine Jay and Tom Patchett wrote and performed in 1971 on *Make Your Own Kind of Music,* a summer-replacement musical variety series starring the Carpenters and the New Doodletown Pipers (someone could make a joke about *that*).

Though Pat Williams would rather be celebrated for such symphonic pieces as *Gulliver,* a collaboration with the playwright Larry Gelbart released in 1988—his bread and butter is television and film composition (it's Pat's music you hear in the ode to Mary Richards, "You're Gonna Make It After All," now an anthem of late-night TV). Fans of *Molly Dodd* still call, wondering if that show's theme song was recorded for distribution (it wasn't). An alumnus of Duke University's jazz band, Pat has been nominated for an Oscar (for his adaptation of Vivaldi in

Breaking Away), for Emmys (winning three times), and he's two-for-sixteen on Grammys.

After *Slap Maxwell* and *Molly Dodd,* Pat knows what to expect from Jay; still, he was taken aback when Jay called about *Smoldering Lust.* "When I heard the title I just laughed. I thought, Oh, great, he's really lost it this time, completely. But then I saw some rough cuts and knew he'd pulled off this very adult program." The two men agreed that the score, from the title song to the incidental background music, had to be played absolutely straight, not in a way that set up or italicized the comedy at all. Its musical themes would be the antithesis of the kind of lilting, zippy tunes that announce gags in a sitcom. The humor, Jay told Pat at the end of June, once the first three shows had completed filming, "will take care of itself. You don't have to think about it."

After his initial talk with Jay, Pat is on his own. He watches episodes repeatedly, "looking *through* the show on a sort of longitudinal curve, to see how the narrative and musical themes can relate. My job is to help hold it all together—the story, the look, the feel." Time spent alone in the studio, broken up by easygoing hours spent with writers he respects and fellow musicians, is to him what his work is all about, but fewer jobs remain this uncomplicated. "Networks have gotten in the way of the creative process. I've never seen so many layers of committee thinking—all these people you have to deal with, constantly." He attributes the mess to the breakdown of studio system. "The studios were like families, and not just for the stars. There were staff musicians, orchestrators, and arrangers, all working in departments overseen by musician executives. Like Lionel Neuman, who ran the music department at Twentieth Century—Fox and could talk to producers and directors in musical terms. Now it's management types who come down to the recording studio, look at the film with you, and say, 'Let's put some note here and there.' And eight different executives are involved in a show, so that'll happen eight different times a day, because none of them can stand to be in the same room with each other.

"After you and the director and the writers and the producers have finally agreed on what the music should be, these people enter and object, citing demographics. Well, I don't write demographics. I write music. Basically I try to entertain people.

"They think this preoccupation with demographics is smart, that it'll result in shows that please everyone. But the real result is shows that don't please anyone."

Not so long ago Pat worked at home at a baby grand, scribbling on score paper to showcase the results for clients, pounding away at the piano as if he were at a Tin Pan Alley audition. "I could get away with that on this job," he says, "knocking out notes and warbling out 'Smoldering Lu-u-ust … ' Jay would get it. But I've had to learn the new tricks, learn to use the latest toys." He's mostly referring to the computer at the studio he shares with other musicians, the Village Recorder, in West Los Angeles. A marvelous toy indeed, the computer can synthesize rattles, drums, string quartets, Brazilian flutes, a sixteenth-century mandolin, harps, bassoons—anything that's plucked, beaten, blown, shaken, stroked, or strummed. Manning the synthesizer's sprawling, twinkling console, which looks like a model of nighttime L.A., is Charles Pollard, who, at thirty-one, looks like the whiz kid he is, a graduate of the acclaimed music school at North Texas State. "Charlie brings something to the party I don't have," says Pat of his partner.

Pat would sometimes still rather be working at home on the piano, but he can't afford to look back: "It's keep up or get out." He points out that the advantage of the new technology is not the savings in time; it still takes about a day to produce four minutes of music, the same as composing by hand. But at the end of a day at the computer, he's got a brilliantly polished result, "an incredible demo tape, something that sounds ready to go on the air."

After a couple of weeks' work, on a cloudy afternoon in mid-July, Pat pops a cassette into a tape player at the Village Recorder and plays the *Smoldering Lust* theme song. It's a torchy piece, something for a smoky lounge. Hearing it for the first time, Jay knows it's right; the tune is good enough, he tells Pat, to release as a single. He has only one concern about the saxophone, which blows heavy in the middle of the song. "Is that sax too—wet, maybe?" he asks Pat, who turns to Charlie, who fiddles with a knob to bring down the sax, dry it out. The theme plays again, from the top. And again. The music fills the room, and Jay smiles as he listens, gets up to stand at an imaginary microphone and sing. "You did it," he tells Pat, who responds by turning the volume even higher, then speaking above the horns: "Now all we need are some words."

> *Smoldering lust*
> *A moth around a flame*
> *Desire in a shameless heart*
>
> *Smoldering lust*
> *The seventh deadly sin*
> *When skin discovers skin*
> *and lips part*
>
> *Wanting what you see*
> *No matter what the cost*
> *Knowing you may be*
> *Permanently lost in lust*
> *Lose yourself you must...*
> *Smoldering lust*

Overwrought and unapologetic about it, the lyrics belong to Arthur Hamilton, whose hyperbolic "Cry Me a River" was a hit when Julie London softly sang it in 1953. A decade later on her debut album, Barbra Streisand reinterpreted the song with a jilted lover's eye-for-an-eye vengeance. Hamilton doesn't have a favorite version. "Julie's is so plaintive," he says. "But when I wrote it I actually thought it was an angry song, so I didn't mind hearing Streisand railing away." Forty years later, "Cry Me a River" continues as "a career in itself," says Arthur, in new recordings by Natalie Cole and Patty Austin. When asked to collaborate on this project, he shares Pat Williams's initial incredulity, asking Pat "Do those two words actually have to appear in the lyrics?" "Not only that," Pat tells him, "but at the top of the song. You can't bury them. They're your key phrase, what all the other words must refer back to." The first line, the first four notes of the song, are the title: "Smol-der-ing lust." Arthur is doubtful: "It's one thing to call a show *Smoldering Lust,* but as a lyricist, rather than use the actual expression, I'd prefer to deal with that as a concept, allude to the feeling. 'Smoldering lust'? How can I write that, build a song around that?" But for the man who imagined a lover crying a river of tears, the task shouldn't be such a stretch.

Reading the first two scripts was all the research Arthur says he needed to do: "You shouldn't get too specific in a theme song because the situations on a show change, characters come and go. I can't make jokes, I can't refer to the foibles of the Codys, can't name them at all, or San Francisco, or private investigators. People will hear the song week after week, so it has to work the sixty-first time as well as the first." With that in mind, and a tape of Pat's music in his Walkman, Arthur boards a plane for New York—he's due at a meeting of ASCAP, the American Society of Composers, Arrangers, and Performers. By the time he lands he's finished the song, seven stanzas jotted on a legal pad. "I don't know why it came to that number of stanzas—one each for the seven deadly sins?" Streaking across the continent, he says, "I started off with those dreaded words, 'Smoldering Lust,' then went carefully, with a moth fluttering around a flame. Then I got a little bolder with 'skin touching skin.' Next I have two people embracing, lips parting. A serious kiss. By the third stanza I was really into it. The emotions ascend, and that's a tricky balance to get; one mistake in the lyrics and the whole song could have fallen apart and sounded ridiculous."

Though playing it straight, Arthur couldn't resist a bit of comic relief in the bridge verse with the words "my fingers sweat." "That's a first for me. I never imagined I'd write a lyric so indelicate. 'Sweat' just isn't one of my words. But the idea of being so wrought up that your fingers are sweating struck me as funny, something to offset the seriousness. The song gets pretty close to the edge, pretty dire. So I got a little silly there."

Hamilton's favorite lines, falling in the fourth stanza,

> *I'm thinking of the clothes*
> *You wear beneath the clothes you wear…*

touch on sexual obsession: "But it's restrained," he says. "I'm trying to convey a subdued or controlled sort of desire—desire across a room, across a table." Such feelings are of course much more up front in the show, and a reference to "the clothes you wear beneath the clothes you wear" isn't at all restrained when Margo tells Brodsky that she wants to "take my underwear off and wrap it around your head."

"Can anyone in the world sing this song but Sue?" Jay asks Pat. Sue is Sue Raney, a singer and voice teacher who cut her first album, a songbook of standards orchestrated by Nelson Riddle, when she was sixteen years old. When she arrives at the Village Recorder to give it a go, Pat relays Jay's question, asking her if she would "rank this among the songs that no one in the world can sing but you." Sue shrugs; it's not as if it's "The Star-Spangled Banner." Pat puts Jay at ease by telling him that she can sing even "The Shadow of Your Smile." "Now there's a tough one," he says. "If she can sing that, she can sing anything."

Sue adores Pat. She's known him since the 1960s, when they were both in New York and he would come to see her open for the likes of Don Rickles and Flip Wilson at the Americana Hotel. Before the first take on the *Smoldering Lust* theme she asks a little about the show, not knowing if it's a comedy or a drama or what. Since the show is a spoof but the song isn't, he advises her to sing it earnestly. Arthur, also on hand for the recording session, adds that the lyrics "should be taken seriously, but not too." It helps to hear that. "The words really drip with sensuality and I don't want to overdo it or be obvious. I don't think I should sound lustful at all." Rehearsing at home, she imagined "elegant people, with the high stakes of lovemaking on their minds." A song like this one, she says, "brings out the actor in me."

Before entering the sound booth, she asks for a cup of peppermint tea. "I'm a little throaty," she says—though that's perhaps not a handicap in singing a song that would almost be more effective if it were whispered. Arthur is excited, telling her that he'll never outgrow the thrill of hearing a singer make his words come alive. Taking her position at the microphone in the deep-sea quiet of the sound booth, Sue looks through the glass separating her from Pat and Charlie, who are seated at the synthesizer console, and from Jay and Arthur, who hover and pace about the control room. Pat calls for silence, then cues Charlie and Sue. The work begins, then stops and starts again, and again, but from the first go everyone knows that singer and song are a luscious match.

Sue is the only critical one present, starting over repeatedly to try other phrasing, soften consonants, lengthen or shorten vowels: "Which sounds warmer? Didn't 'lose yourself' sound better this time? Can I try that '-st' at the end of the first 'lust' again? Am I *singing* it too much, or not enough?" Phrases and words can be "punched in," with fixes spliced onto the master tape, but Pat discourages Sue from fussing over it. "Don't perfect it too much," he says.

❧ ❧ ❧

After the title song is cut, individual episodes must be "spotted" with music cues. Watching edited shows on a television monitor, Pat, Charlie, and Jay discuss what kind of music should go where, note by note, scene by scene, zipping through each episode in about an hour. Describing the music behind Chris's discovery of the dead body in Room 1216, Jay asks that it be "foreboding and tense but also romantic. Terrifying, really, but let's not tip it off—I don't want it to sound like we're gonna see a dead girl. I mean, we do, there's blood all over the place. But it should all look and sound strangely beautiful." Charlie comes up with a jumpy plucking of strings, mixed with a few nervous wooden rattles—an edge-of-your-seat effect that's just right.

More akin to a movie than a sitcom, the show uses music to help define character and enhance mood. Today the signature themes for Brodsky and Cookie are being addressed, musical signatures to cue the characters' comings and goings and give hints of their interior lives. Brodsky's theme, a few fidgety notes on a muted horn, is appropriate accompaniment to the mental wanderings of this chronically horny drifter. Cookie's theme also clues us in to her sexual feelings, but in an altogether different way, with a strange synthesized woodwind that spirals up like a siren. It's an exotic call, and Charlie lays it into the soundtrack to signal Chris's belated discovery of the sensual woman hiding beneath the overalls and bookworm glasses. When the flutey notes rise, off come Cookie's glasses and down comes her long black hair.

The spotting sessions continue all summer. To exaggerate the romance of a flashback to Margo and Chris's courtship days, Jay asks Pat and Charlie for "a sort of Renoir or Monet sound, whatever that would be," and Charlie gets it with a few clear notes from the computer samples labeled "french horn" and "violin." Watching Eve sashay down an office hallway Pat wonders if they should go for a "da-da-*da*" or a "*da*-da-da." The latter wins.

And so the show's moods are lightened or darkened, sweetened or soured. The score lengthens. It's a lot of sound for a half-hour program; at one session Jay wonders aloud, "Are we going over the top with all this music? Are we scoring this show to death?" But Pat is delighted: "It's like we're doing a movie. We're getting symphonic."

Subsequent scoring sessions will add live music to the synthesized foundation. Pat looks forward to this part of the process, though the show's lean budget allows him only two musicians. "I wish I could call in a dozen players," he says, "and get them here much earlier in the process." But his dilemma is no different from that of any other freelance composer in town who's been forced to automate. "The technology I've had to invest in to stay competitive is putting musicians out of work." He once would hire as many as thirty-five musicians for a scoring session; now, says Pat, "I count myself lucky to be able to get these two guys to do some sweetening for me."

The soundtrack needs real horns, and Pat has called in Gary Foster, a saxophone player, and trumpeter Warren Leuning, who squeeze in this gig while working on another, better paying one, as orchestra members on Barbra Streisand's second Broadway album. Television has kept them busy for years (Warren was one of Lawrence Welk's Champagne Music Makers). If work ever looked like fun, this scoring session is it. Poised with their instruments in the sound booth, Gary and Warren wait for instructions from Pat, Charlie, and Jay, who are watching an episode on the monitor. Chris has entered Eve's dressing room, where she is casually changing her blouse (and bra) and telling him that she wants him "more than pizza."

PAT: "Pretty hot stuff for television. Should we change the attitude a little?"

JAY: "What do you mean, 'attitude'?"

PAT: "Well, it's sexy and all, but maybe it could use a little be-bop. Or cool it down a bit."

JAY: "I don't know what you mean, but go for it."

PAT: (over the intercom, to Warren) "Can you lighten this up here, Warren? Try anything."

JAY: "Make it chilly."

WARREN: "Okay if I have to add a note or two to get that? How many seconds do I get on the clock?"

PAT: "Don't worry about it."

A clear ribbon of sound rises from the clarinet.

JAY: "That's nice; that's Cody's blissfully ignorant side. Cody—the man who wants something but doesn't know what, and wouldn't know how to express it even if he did know."

For two hours, Gary and Warren work with Pat to make the show sing. "We focus on the show," says Pat, "on the look and the sound of it, and that's the only reason I'm here. If you can stay on that as a composer, it feels terrific, but it also meets the ultimate bottom-line question of the recording business. Which is, Did the money get into the album? Often it doesn't; it goes for everything else. But we got the best, richest sound possible. What money we did have, we spent well. It got into the album."

The sounds of *Smoldering Lust* (the phrase could almost be the title of one of the self-consciously cool instrumental LPs of the fifties) are a good match for the noir-ish mood of the show, but viewers probably shouldn't make too much of the union. "You know this foreboding music we've made here?" Jay announces as the musicians pack up at the end of the final scoring session. "It's a smokescreen. It's a smokescreen to disguise what's really going on in this show." And that, he offers—borrowing the absurdist raison d'être of *Seinfeld*—"is absolutely nothing."

CHAPTER TWELVE
HUDDLE

Each of the production periods for the series (there are four, with three shows each, plus one at summer's end to total thirteen episodes) is preceded by a sort of round-table free-for-all where everything anyone will possibly need is discussed, debated, begged for, denied, okayed, laughed at, applauded: locations, construction, costumes, hair and makeup styles, props, set decorations, the hiring of extras, special effects. Everything. Speak up now for a wild wall for Chris's office and the extra hand in the cabinet shop to build it—a sweater or two to give the impression that Margo has a fall wardrobe—a haircut for Eve—an expensive crane for the camera—an extra day at the health club shoot—an extra hand in the cabinet shop. Oh, and for Cookie's vending-machine lunch, Maggie Han has asked for a turkey sandwich on whole wheat with a little mayo; David Glazer will prepare a few.

A half dozen cafeteria tables borrowed from the commissary are set up end to end in the wide-open space of the production office reception area. Presto: an instant conference room. Shows seven, eight, and nine are on the agenda for the third production meeting, held on August 6. Presiding are Jay, who will direct show seven, set in the hotel ballroom, and Peter Baldwin, who will direct the other two shows.

Show eight opens with a medium-length shot of a vandal spraying green paint on Margo's office wall and Peter wants to know what the graffiti should look like. "A mask, sort of," says

Rick. Russ wrote the episode, but he's left the day-to-day work of *Smoldering Lust* for the Linda Lavin sitcom, *Room for Two*, so Rick is shepherding the script through production.

Ann Champion speaks up for a wild or removable wall: "We'll need an extra one on standby, to use while we're cleaning the other between takes." She makes a note to call Mike Wright in the wood shop, saying that she'll ask him to do it "fast and cheap." David asks what kind of paint to get. "Not paint," Ann says. "Hairspray. Get green hairspray—it'll clean easier."

Something else for Mike and the hammer crew: Monday's shoot in the hotel hallway will be the final one for that set, so they can strike it that evening. "And can we start thinking about building Cody's cabin there?" asks Ann.

"Right," says Steve Wertimer, the assistant director, who admits that he "lives for little details," which is what A.D.'s do, backing up directors.

"What about the guy who comes in to clean the wall?" Peter asks, thinking about the extra actor. "I think he should be an older guy."

"Do you want him in overalls?" asks Lani Reynolds.

"Maybe a khaki shirt and pants—a janitor's uniform," says Peter.

"He should wear lots of keys on his belt, too," adds Steve. "Janitors have jillions of keys."

As usual, some oddball props are needed for a Cody Canyon photoshoot, this one featuring Eve in full Pocahontas drag. "Where can we get a tepee?" Steve asks Ruth Bracken. "Oh, they're all over town," she says. "I can rent one at Roscity. How many days do we keep it? And what about a background—is this a cowboys-and-Indians thing?"

"Big-time background," says Steve. "Rocks, boulders, canyons... Can you do a backdrop?"

"What about the jacuzzi scene?" Ann wants to know, referring to two days' shooting scheduled at the Woodland Hills

Marriott. "Any suggestions for turning a hotel pool and gym into a fancy old men's club?"

"I'll bring in some palms," says Ruth. "And can we shade those windows—a private men's spa should be sort of dark, shouldn't it?"

Jay speaks up for the first time. "What else can we do to make it look right? What about signs that say 'Locker Room' or 'Massage Room'?"

"Piles of white towels?" asks Ruth.

Someone points out that the scene will require the actors, John Calvin and whoever Cheryl Bayer finds to play a liberal but corrupt Senator, to spend hours in hot water. "Literally," says Steve Wertimer. "Ouch. Can we turn down the chlorine?" Liz Matthews says she'll arrange it.

An important point from Lani: if the show goes on the air in late June or early July 1993, as the latest rumor has it, this batch of shows will bring the characters into the first weeks of autumn. "But they may need fall clothes," she says. "I'll get Margo and Eve some sweaters. And colors—we'll need to get some fall colors."

Liz and Steve Confer talk briefly about the exterior of the Codys' house, which has only recently been found. There had been a couple of good candidates, a Victorian mansion in San Marino, a shingled house near the ocean, but both fell through: one because the owner asked for too much money, the other because the block association objected, citing the disruption and chaos that camera crews bring. Liz found the house smack in the middle of Los Angeles, in Echo Park. It's a beauty—built in the early twentieth century, with bay windows and turrets, and nicely restored to its original splendor. Equally important to Liz is that it's "film-crew friendly"—the owners and neighbors actually welcome the disruption of filmmaking. The owners of the house charge rent, and the block association charges a daily fee; Liz will also have to secure no less than five city permits to bring in the necessary trailers, lights, crane, and trucks and to arrange parking for cast and crew.

Steve Confer approves of the find, telling Liz that all he needs to do with the camera is to "establish the house and push-in"—that is, a long shot to set up the basic location, a house on a residential block, then a zoom to take viewers to the front door. "If the details aren't perfect," he says, "don't worry about it."

Jay is eager to discuss the next episode he'll direct, number seven, which returns to the scene of the crime, the Park Plaza Hotel. He has ambitious plans for the episode. "This is gonna be real moviemaking" says Jay. "I want the camera on a crane and in constant motion. One long take." His inspiration, he doesn't mind admitting, is the opening shot of Orson Welles's *Touch of Evil*. "Can you do that?" he asks Steve. "Track everybody as they enter the ballroom, then just pull back and up sort of, and glide over to someone else. From Brodsky to Margo and Chris to Eve and Philip ... " The long roving shot requires an unusual amount of preparation on Steve's part: before he sits behind the camera, he'll have to mirror-match every movement of the crane-mounted camera—left, right, up, down—with those of the actors. Like Jay, he's giddy about the chance to do what real moviemakers do. "Hold your breath," he says. "It's going to be gorgeous."

It's going to be expensive, too. Besides the crane, they'll need lots of extras. Suzanne Miller has arrived late to the meeting from TBS Casting, the show's source for actors in nonspeaking parts. Randy Suhr, who is responsible for wrangling all the seen-but-not-heard extras, has already prepared a five-page "Extras Breakdown" listing such parts as Customers, Hostesses, Busboys, Phone Woman, Waiters, Salesman, Bartenders, Photographers. The general meeting ends and Lani, who must dress the extras, and David, who must provide them with props, stay on with Randy and Suzanne to marshal these human forces.

"Jay doesn't like to seem fussy about the extras, but he does care," David says to Suzanne. "Last time at the hotel he was going around complaining that the people couldn't act. They were supposed to look like this tony, moneyed crowd, and he thought some of them looked like slobs. And there's that one guy you sent over who's kind of deformed, with a tiny little head. Jay doesn't want him again." Randy adds a word about "some blonde who kept worming her way into every shot. We've got to watch out for her."

The episode calls for a band. Randy asks Suzanne if she can't find extras who actually play musical instruments, enough "so that it looks like they're making real sounds." And as for the photographers in the crowd scene, David asks, "Can you make sure they know how to use a thirty-five-millimeter camera? We had a couple of guys in the first show who were fumbling around so much you knew they were handling props."

Lani has the last word, telling Suzanne about the wardrobe shift: "We're planning for fall clothes now. Sweaters and scarves would be fine for extras out in the hotel lobby."

No formal adjournment is called, no final cheer. The huddle breaks up and the production meetings end quietly, with people wandering off to begin the enormous task at hand, pulling together all the elements for another three shows.

Listening to every word is Tony Carey of Brillstein-Grey, who looks like no one's idea of a bottom-line watchdog. Wearing his blond hair to his shoulders, dressed in jeans and cowboy boots, Tony could be mistaken for a crew member when he shows up at Empire to "make sure the money gets spent the way it's supposed to be spent," as he describes his job. At the outset of production, Tony suggested finding one person to do double duty as director of photography and camera operator. The hiring of Steve Confer, who came on board in such a two-for-one deal, saves the production around $3,000 a week. "Not much," Tony admits, "but it adds up. We scrimp and save wherever we can."

When Jay's homage to *Touch of Evil* goes alarmingly over budget, Tony brings in Judy Gordon, an ace show accountant, to review the figures with Harriette Ames-Regan, the unit production manager, who has denied little to the producers, okaying Jay's entire wish list: two hundred extras, the crane for the camera, a ten-piece band, three extra lights at $500 each, trailers for wardrobe and hair and makeup, dressing rooms, security guards, decorations for the ballroom. Harriette's previous television experience was coordinating scripts for the shortlived *Julie Andrews Hour,* so Judy may feel she is broaching a new idea to her when she explains the most important function of unit production managers. Which is: "to say no." Whenever anyone asks for anything extra—the gaffer for more lights, the grip for extra tools and more bodies to use them, a producer for additional days on location—the unit manager must say no. "*Then* you start to negotiate," says Judy.

As the tally for show seven approaches the million-dollar mark, Judy goes white. The episode is more than $200,000 over budget, and that money, according to the contract, must come from the producers—Brillstein-Grey and Jay. "Either that," Judy says, "or we have to take that much from another show's budget." But that can't be done until more shows are written and the company knows what it will need in the way of locations, sets, props, and other elements. Though the producers have agreed in good faith to be financially responsible for the show, they have no intention of bankrolling this whopping excess. And so Judy and Harriette and Tony sit down with legal pads and calculators and start to say no: first to the five days' shooting, cutting it to three. Then to a three-day rental of the camera crane, slashing it to one (at $1,500 per day, the cost falls $3,000). Then to the two hundred extras, telling Lani and Randy to make do with seventy-five. Then no to Bill Witthens, insisting that he hire just two extra hands, not four. And so on, until they've cut more than $175,000; the remaining overrun is manageable now and can be made up easily enough in subsequent episodes.

The trimming doesn't show on-screen. Jay gets the fluid, swooping camera effect and the ballroom seems mobbed with guests, all stylishly dressed in black. The band members, though not professional musicians, convincingly mime the playing of instruments. What the viewer doesn't see are the long hours that went into the three-day shoot: the desperate dressing up of the extras, the pre-dawn preparation of the shabby ballroom with rigs of lights, cans of paint, and yards of cheap fabric.

Back in Beverly Hills, Tony checks balance sheets while eyeing the handsome final product on a video monitor in his office. "We're producing this show very well," he says. "And we're coming in at about where we should on the numbers." Working on more than one production, Tony learns to piggyback some services and expenses, such as set and costume storage and rentals of equipment and trucks. Different shows can even share cleanup crews. "Like anything, it's cheaper by the dozen," says Tony, who has made a cooperative prop-storage deal for *Smoldering Lust*, the canceled *Dennis Miller Show,* and *The Larry Sanders Show.*

In the eyes of most around Empire, the money spent on *Smoldering Lust* passes the ultimate test of film production: it shows on the screen. The credit goes to the million-dollar work performed by Steve at the camera, Lani in wardrobe, and Ann, Lori, and Ruth in design and decoration. They've pulled some beautiful rabbits out of a cheap hat.

CHAPTER THIRTEEN
BRADLEY AND THE J WORD

Dave Brodsky stumbles into Margo Cody's closet, flicks a cigarette lighter, and holds the flame aloft in order to peek around. "You're probably wondering what I'm doing in here," he says. Bradley Whitford is wondering the same thing. Staring into the cold eye of the camera, the actor freezes up, suddenly realizing that even in a worst-ratings scenario a few million people will be watching this performance. An experienced stage actor who prides himself on having a "good hard skeleton" of dramatic technique and training, Bradley is accustomed to weeks of rehearsals, to knowing his character inside out before facing an audience. This afternoon, his first day on *Smoldering Lust,* he is doing the closing monologue from the third episode; earlier in the day he shot his first scene with Kate Capshaw and John Calvin, in the Codys' bedroom. He met the other leads just yesterday, in the hallway outside their dressing rooms. *What,* he wonders, *am I doing in here?* The confidence that was so manifest in his audition is gone. He feels almost angry—at Jay, for not giving him more direction; at himself, for not demanding more rehearsal time. Suddenly he calls a halt to the scene. "Gotta catch my breath," he mutters. He feels like apologizing—to Jay, who is directing the episode, to Steve Confer who is perched on the other side of that scary cyclops of a camera, to all the grips and the gaffer, to Petra Jorgensen, the script supervisor.

"The crew probably thought I was being a temperamental New York actor," says Bradley, who attributes the attack to a kind of stage fright brought on by a delayed reaction to his good fortune in landing the role of Brodsky. It's not just the money he's making, which is staggering enough to a midwestern boy of modest upbringing accustomed to Actors Equity scale. This crack at the big time could provide the ingredient that's been missing in his career—exposure, the "visibility" his agent Nevin Dolcefino harps on as being essential to an actor's graduation to bigger roles in television and, ultimately, film. The Michael J. Fox-Robin Williams-Tom Hanks success story. But Bradley isn't thinking movie-stardom, not now anyway. "You know what a TV role like Brodsky means to an actor like me?" he says. "Besides more movies, it means that I could now do *Hamlet* at the Guthrie. That's how star-fucky the world's become."

Bolstered by a quick cup of black coffee ("It shouldn't work, but it does," says Bradley, who has developed his own "caffeine-abuse method of acting"), he returns to the set and gets through the day "without ever getting a grip on what I was supposed to be doing." But by the end of the week he's hit his stride as Brodsky, around whom the show revolves. That Brodsky is an embodiment of Jay is evident to all on set, as is the creator's fondness for the actor.

On location all of the following week at the Park Plaza Hotel, Bradley is the center of attention in Brodsky's silly but snappy red-and-black bellboy outfit. The bigness of the production amazes him—the catering, the number of lights, the crew members crawling over scaffolding, the more than one hundred extras milling about the grand ballroom, the street closed off to traffic to make way for the actors' trailers. Besides shooting a pointed exchange with John at the elevator this week, Bradley must also do the furtive kissing scene with Kate at a bank of telephones off the lobby. After plenty of jokes of the it's-a-tough-job-but-someone's-got-to-do-it variety, Bradley decides what he'll tell a reporter from *GQ* who arrives on the set to interview Jay: "If she asks me what I do on the show, I'll tell her it's my job to kiss Kate." It's hard to believe that the cocky Bradley of this and the following fifteen weeks of shooting is the same rattled actor who lost his cool in Margo's closet. "Actually," he says, "it took me all of two days to go from total existential panic to raving narcissism."

Excited word starts to circulate about Bradley, suggestions that his Brodsky could be his big break. He's fabulous, he's told. So gigantically likable. And then it's uttered, the *F* word: *Famous.* "I really think this could make him a star," says Rick Dresser. "He's going to be famous," says Jay. Many such comments get back to Bradley. No actor so new to television should hear something like that, even one of Bradley's talent and charm. What if the show doesn't fly? The work may never even get on the air.

Toward the end of the summer, when NBC invites a camera crew from the E-channel to come shoot a behind-the-scenes story, the focus is on Kate. When the reporter does point the microphone toward Bradley, her one question is a coy one about Kate: "What's it like to kiss Mrs. Spielberg?" On his toes, Bradley yawns an answer: "Oh, is that who Kate is married to?"

In spite of the in-house hoopla about him, Bradley seems reluctant to take his craft or even this particular enterprise seriously. The summer's headlines engage him far more deeply than those in the trade papers. When he does talk about actors and acting it is almost always facetiously. To his co-stars such talk sounds like heresy, but Kate can't help whooping when he remarks that the actors are nothing more than "dogs in a dog show." He elaborates: "They keep us in these kennels, which are our dressing rooms, then trot us out to do our tricks. We go into the ring, jump through the hoops, we're given a treat, then led back to our dressing rooms." Recalling auditions, he darkens the metaphor: "It's like being in a dog pound. If you sit in your cage quietly trembling, the people you want to notice you will ignore you. The idiots doing flips at the front of the cage are the ones who get chosen. If you stay in back, shying away, you get inciner- ated. So you've got to get up front and do your flips."

Having to report to makeup at dawn all summer long sounded like torture at first, but Bradley learns to love it. He looks for- ward to "rolling out of bed, and have someone touch my face and stroke my hair while I'm practically in a dream state. They sort of gently prod me into character." To him, Diane Biggs and Paula Sutor in hair and makeup are the "sensual sensors of the show. They know everything about the real you in there, not just about the character. It's all in your eyes. On Mondays, I swear, they can tell how many times you made love over the weekend." After his good experiences on the show, Bradley can understand why an actor would insist on always having his own makeup person. Kate agrees. "Next feature film offer I get," she says, "it'll take me about three seconds to say, 'Please, may I bring along Paula?' "

Flipping through record albums in Brodsky's shop one after- noon, Bradley has what he thinks is a better idea for a scene in show three, which is being directed by Jay. "Shouldn't I stop at the bottom of the stairs and look toward the camera just for a second before I go over to the records?" he asks. Jay listens with half an ear, then says, "The trouble with actors often is that they're smart. Like you. Funny, quick, intuitive—all those things that make you good at what you do. When actors have problems I really ought to listen to them. But I've come to realize that they're always incredibly self-serving. Now what was *your* problem?" Bradley lets the matter drop, ceding a victory to Jay in their ongoing con- test of wits. Late one evening, arriving to dub a few lines over the dialogue track at EFX, a recording studio in Burbank, Bradley doesn't fail to let Jay know what inconvenience he is suffering: "This is a pain," he says. "And you know, I never have to do this with other directors I work with. They all get it right the first time."

After being directed by Jay in the first three episodes, then by Lesli Glatter, Bradley has difficulty enduring for two weeks in August the heavy hand of Peter Baldwin, who has been hired to direct episodes eight and nine. Jay and Lesli trust and truly like actors; Peter does not project those sentiments, and his temper is on a short fuse, sometimes exploding in angry outbursts. He is particularly sharp with an extra, a man in his sixties, hired to scrub graffiti from Margo's office wall. Though not nimble, the man is more than competent and cooperative, and the cast and crew look stunned when Peter yells at him continually for moving so slowly. "That sweet man," says Kate. "Why does Peter have to be so mean to him? What's the big deal—how can you wash down a wall wrong?" Bradley's problems with Peter have to do with his deliberate, inch-by-inch style of direction. Working for Peter, the actor feels like a marionette. "Instead of just telling me to enter a room and flip on the light switch, Peter goes, 'First come through the doorway on your right foot—*make sure you enter on the right foot*—then begin to flex your left shoulder muscle, bringing your hand up to a forty-five-degree angle to your torso. Now slowly extend your index finger toward the switch ... ' Geez, how can an actor work like that? You know what that does to you? It sucks the zen out of you."

"My reps coming over today," Bradley crows one afternoon midway through production. Such calls are a standard courtesy, a way for agents to show support for their clients. Today at Empire, with Nevin meeting Bradley in Brodsky's record store and Maggie Han having lunch in her dressing room with Robert Brown, her agent from J. Michael Bloom, it feels like Parents' Day.

"What's famous?" says Bradley. "All it means is that if you crack a little joke people will laugh too hard at it, that you're forgiven transgressions and bad behavior because of who you are, that you can get away with being a lousy friend." By the first of September *Smoldering Lust* is in its last weeks of production, and Bradley has tired of the question about what the show might do for his career. The series will wrap—complete all shooting—in less than three weeks, and NBC hasn't given any hints about an air date. No one at the network, in fact, has said anything about the show since early in the summer. Bradley's future is no longer where he thought it was, in Jay's hands, but in those of the network programming people. He of course desperately wants the show to get a strong time slot and a juicy promotional budget. And he wouldn't mind if the show made him what he prefers to call "a little bit known," though he sees a downside to that, saying that *Smoldering Lust* could "typecast me as a comic. Then whatever else I do, audiences will expect me to be funny. I'd pick up the skull in *Hamlet* and get a laugh. That's the part about TV that scares me—people start associating you with one kind of role, start thinking you can do only one thing."

After shooting his last scene, Bradley is back where his journey began when he auditioned at the St. James's Club. This time, here for a poolside dinner, he wonders how the production might be different when—if—the network renews the series. "I'm afraid it'll all be changed, it won't be the way it has been, like a bunch of renegades doing something new and different." The show hasn't come close to venturing into the experimental or avant-garde, of course, but it has maintained its independence from the network, and Bradley loves that spirit. Whether there will be a price to pay for that independence remains to be seen: hands off during production may mean apathetic programming and promotion, too.

Until Bradley knows what the network's plans are for the show, he cannot make long-range plans of his own. For now he has work in three high-profile films: Jonathan Demme's *Philadelphia*, the Clint Eastwood-Kevin Costner film, *A Perfect World*, and *My Life*, starring Michael Keaton. Pondering the unknown future of *Smoldering Lust* sends him into a spin, but for now a piece of Jay's jaded brand of wisdom sets him straight. "This show's not going anywhere, Bradley," Jay told him early on in production. "Even if it does, all we'll get is thirteen more. And even if it does take off and runs for years and you become a huge success, remember this: If you're a success in television, then there's probably something seriously wrong with you."

CHAPTER FOURTEEN
PLAYING MARGO

No one at Empire pretends not to know who Kate Capshaw is. *Indiana Jones and the Temple of Doom*, after all, one of the all-time moneymaking films, made her a household name, even before she married its director. And so Jay's initial hesitation about working with her was echoed around Empire: Will she be difficult? Will she expect star treatment? What is she doing in this dump, anyway? Along with the doubts came the equally expected gushing about her status in the industry, as if she were Norma Shearer to Spielberg's Irving Thalberg (the parallel is weak: Spielberg doesn't fashion vehicles for his wife as Thalberg did as head of production at MGM). Still, her presence graces *Smoldering Lust* and causes some commotion, infusing the day-to-day business with a touch of Hollywood royalty.

Two days before shooting begins, Kate has a makeup test, meeting Steve Confer for the first time. The director of photography prides himself on knowing how to photograph women, their faces and bodies—to pick up extra cash, he sometimes shoots soft-porn videos for Playboy—and he can't believe his good fortune with Kate. "Blue-green eyes, a hint of red in her hair, that creamy skin," he says. "You can't go wrong with a woman who looks like that."

Kate knows she is in good hands with Steve, and feels the same way about Paula Sutor, the show's makeup artist, who likes to describe the human face as a canvas. "I was studying painting," she says, discussing how she got started in the business, "but the biggest influence on my career came from my college roommate. He was a transvestite and asked me one day to do his makeup. After a few times I realized it was just like what I was doing in school, creating optical illusions, making things seem larger or smaller, with shadows and light. Only instead of doing it with paint, you do it with makeup."

Paula is in the Codys' bedroom, touching up Kate between her tumbles with Bradley on the floor. She and Diane Briggs stand by during every take, ready to rush over with hairbrushes and combs, powders and pancake, complexion brushes and sprays, all of which they carry around in holsters like quick-on-the-draw gunfighters. Continuity of appearance is as vital as wardrobe continuity: if Bradley's hair is hanging down over one eye after Kate nibbles an ear, then Diane must make sure it's doing the same thing when the scene resumes.

"It's a matter of bringing out all the the good elements that are already there," says Diane about styling Kate's reddish brown mane in a simple, chin-length cut that recalls Garbo's. Paula uses complexion tones to match the hair with a palette that's "very natural for Kate, only enhanced. Basically I keep her in the same rusty sort of color all through the show. Warm hues bring out the blue in her eyes. I try not to make her too pink, no pinker than what she gets when she pinches her cheeks. Somehow that's too girly for Margo."

For her first day of shooting, Kate had asked for a car and driver. "Oh, God, it's starting," Jay grumbled to Bernie Brillstein, fearing the worst was coming true about Mrs. Spielberg. Bernie tells him to calm down; it's a long drive from Pacific Palisades to Burbank and it's only this once. Besides, she's asked for a sedan, not a limousine. Though accustomed to the luxuries afforded by big-budget films, Kate is delighted with the low-budget enterprise at Empire and finds the lack of niceties in the upstairs production offices touching. "Have you noticed the 'in' message box at Michele's desk?" she asks Bradley, referring to the show's receptionist, Michele Ceazan. "It's made out of a cereal box—Wheaties, I think—with these handmade cardboard dividers." To her, *Smoldering Lust* is positively bohemian, "like we're scraping together something in the East Village." If the show is a success and the production regroups for another season, Kate would hate to lose any of its sweet, unspoiled quality. "I want the operation to stay exactly as it is," she tells Bradley. Then she reconsiders a detail or two: "Except I'd like a window in my dressing room, that's all I ask. Oh, and the carpeting—it's so ugly you could throw up. And I'd love to shoot on the west side, close to home."

After her first-day escort to the studio, Kate has the route down, making the forty-five-minute journey in her Volvo station wagon. She runs her lines while driving to work, glancing at the day's pages clipped onto the dashboard. The morning readings are important, for Kate has trouble getting a grip on Margo, claims for weeks she has "no idea who my character is." Jay's silence on the matter is intimidating. As producer, writer, and director, he'd rather not be bothered with an actor's struggles. And though Kate would like to interpret that as confidence in her, "I can't be sure," she says. Kate reports to makeup at 7:30 A.M. and is on the set by 8:15 to deliver, in bed with John Calvin, such absurdities as: "So that's it, then. You've decided to strap our marriage into a chair and yank its teeth out, like a heartless periodontist." With little more than a weekend to prepare for this scene, Kate feels as if she's up on a high wire without a net but, surprising herself, appreciates the precariousness of her position. "I haven't had enough time to get overconfident," she says, "and maybe there's just enough time to hit a little bit of the truth."

The scariest part to Kate is the sense that she's working out Margo's puzzles on camera. Because her casting was down to the wire there is no time for actual rehearsals but only technical walk-throughs. Margo's career, Kate realizes, is not one of the character's big concerns; the Cody business runs itself. Her focus is on the men in her life, on romance. As the series unfolds and the increasingly frustrated Margo reveals a kinship with Maggie of *Cat on a Hot Tin Roof,* Kate hopes that the character's conflicting desires will be resolved. "If this show goes, Margo's got to look at her relationships and decide which one she wants. She's wound up a really lonely lady. When she's in front of Cody, she's acutely aware of their history, of where they once were, where they are now. She can grab Brodsky, kiss him, then slap him— and she's terrified of what she'd become if she allowed passion to take over her life." Kate is chomping to let Margo loose, to give viewers a lascivious reason to tune in.

"In some ways, Margo is very young," she tells Bradley in one of their end-of-the-day dressing room chats. "She acts on her impulses, and she has good instincts. It shows in the Cody business, which she didn't have to really work at to make happen. I think it's a complete accident that Cody Canyon is a success. It just came naturally for her." She understands how that can happen, she says, because of her husband's example. "A lot of people talk about Steven's success as a filmmaker, but because I know him, I know that his success was incidental. There was only one thing Steven could ever do, and that was to direct a movie. Growing up, he couldn't be successful dating girls, or playing football, or being the most popular kid. There were all these things he couldn't be. The only thing he could be was what he's become. Making movies is where all his stuff is.

"Not to make a direct analogy, but the same is true of Margo when she goes, 'Let's do a—uh—let's do a catalog! ... We'll have pictures and it'll be all this wilderness stuff!' Margo doesn't even know what she's doing, that it's good or big, she has no career plan; it all just happens because it's the only thing she can do. If she had planned on success, it wouldn't have happened, and that's really true in life. If you make it a goal to break box-office records or if you plan to become a star, then it's not going to happen."

Spielberg visits the set just once, when cast and crew are sweating out a street location shoot on a ninety-degree July afternoon. The gesture is gracious but of course also disruptive: an industry deity has come to call. For several days afterward, questions and braggadocio fly: "Did you see Spielberg today?" "He spoke to me!" "What did he say to Jay?" "He looked right at me. I just smiled." "He said how much he liked the scripts." "He asked me about the lights."

Spielberg tells Jay he likes the few scripts he's read, which may have inspired Jay to give Kate a line to play with in a late episode about the "lost ark" (as in *Raiders of…*) of the Cody marriage. As he gets to know her better, Jay even takes to teasing her about her wealth. "You know why she's doing this show? She's bored. She's tired of staying home, looking at all those Monets and Manets. She'd started to redecorate the Xerox room." When NBC is rumored to be for sale, Jay tells Kate to tell her husband to buy the network. *"He* should buy it," he says. "Then you can do nice things for *Smoldering Lust."*

"Jay, they're asking eight billion dollars," Kate replies.

"So?"

One afternoon the inevitable happens to this spouse of a famous director when a crew member approaches Kate as she steps off the set. "Hey, Kate," he says, "I've written a screenplay. Would you show it to Steven for me?" The nervy intrusion, and the use of Spielberg's first name are jarring, but Kate doesn't miss a beat. "Oh, I don't get involved with any of that," she says. "I'm not his business partner. I'm only his girlfriend. If a script comes to our house it does a quick loop around the driveway and goes over to his office at Amblin."

But the crewman is quick too. "I've called—Amblin doesn't accept unsolicited screenplays."

"You don't have an agent?"

"Nope."

So Kate mentions someone, a producer at Amblin who is practically a household name, prominently listed in all of the company's screen credits. She then turns away, rolls her eyes, and heads to her dressing room.

Kate's biography could read like a fanzine chronicle of a starlet's exaggerated rise from rags to riches. The nutshell is that Kathy Sue Nail was born in Texas and raised in Missouri, took a college degree in education, and for several years taught children with learning disabilities. By then she had married a fellow teacher, Robert Capshaw. Their daughter, Jessica, was born in 1977. But Kate grew restless in Missouri, and decided to do something about her daydreams of being an actress, which she had had since the sixth grade, when she played Annie Sullivan in a school production of *The Miracle Worker*. She was told she was pretty and had good legs; what about modeling as a first step to acting? Going along with the plan, her husband snapped some pictures in their backyard, a chain-link fence in the background. Off to New York the family went, and while Robert and Jessica waited on a park bench on East Fifty-ninth Street, beneath the roar of traffic on the "Feelin' Groovy" bridge, Kate made her way through the offices of the Eileen Ford modeling agency. "I was referred from one desk to the next," she says, "and it felt like I was going deeper and deeper into the agency, from one level to the next. I finally got to Eileen herself." If anyone noticed that Kate was an inch shorter than she claimed to be on her résumé, it didn't matter. Ford offered Kate not only a contract but a place to live, an extraordinary perk enjoyed by the lucky lovelies upon signing with the (maternalistic) Ford Agency. The new-to-New York living arrangement sounded like something out of a Jacqueline Susanne novel, but Kate explained to Ford that she had a husband and a baby girl waiting for her outside. Back in Missouri, the Capshaws had a big garage sale before starting a new life in New York.

Madison Avenue kept Kate busy blowing out birthday candles for Certs, leaping into the air for Toyota, and whispering confidences about Tampax. While her modeling career thrived, though, her marriage soured. Soon Kate was single again. All models say they want to act, and Ford didn't listen to Kate's requests to be sent out on auditions. So she switched to another agency, J. Michael Bloom Ltd., which did send her around. She suffered the usual humiliations of the trade, "but I tried to make a little game of it," she says. "I'd pretend that I was the only one they really wanted to see that day, that they were seeing the other actresses just because they had to. *I* was the one they were waiting for and excited about. That's the only way I could go in and get through it. Otherwise, if I thought about the odds, I'd be so disgusted I'd just be surly during the interview." But then she got lucky, landing a recurring role on *One Life to Live*. It wasn't exciting, playing a dying actress on a soap opera, but the work paid so well that she could now treat herself and Jessica to meals out. Her first feature role followed, in *A Little Sex* (and the role—of a woman involved with a philanderer—now seems like preparation for *Smoldering Lust).*

The film that made it happen for Kate, *Indiana Jones,* also caused her enormous grief. Mainstream critics were not kind: Gene Siskel called her a "whining deadhead," adding that when her character, Willie Scott, is dangled over molten lava, "we wish she would fall in." But the heaviest flack came from feminists, who were outraged by Willie's helplessness. Hounded "all over the world," Kate recalls with a chill, she cut short the press tour for the movie. "I was getting absolutely killed and finally said, Relax, will you? You're wasting your breath on a B movie. It's an adventure, it's popcorn, it's for Saturday afternoon. Just stop it."

Because her work in Ridley Scott's *Black Rain* was not widely seen, Kate would like to think that her quiet portrayal of Margo Cody will surprise people. The character may be hopelessly confused about the men in her life, but Margo is not bossed by them, and there isn't a girlish bone in her body. She is a mature, intense woman, with a measured way of speaking, of thinking out loud. If the camera loves Kate's eyes and skin tones, the microphone loves her voice. Her muted tones may remind some of Faye Dunaway's rich mumble in *Chinatown*—as if the actress is speaking with precious stones in her mouth.

Kate's value to *Smoldering Lust* is obvious—not only because of her marquee name, but because she is so—yes, likable—as Margo. As episodes are completed and delivered to NBC, the programming and marketing men—and they virtually all are men, in their forties and fifties—may hate the show but are enthralled by Kate, an actress they haven't seen or thought about for nearly a decade. "*That's* Kate Capshaw?" says programming chief Preston Beckman, once he's finally made time to pop an episode into his VCR. "I can't believe it. She's fantastic." Subtext: *We've got to get her in something that people are going to watch.* Brandon Tartikoff, though gone from NBC, has sneaked a peek at an episode, and pronounces Kate its key to success: "If people can relate to her, it'll go. If not, it's dead." Though Kate is unscathed, the early, mostly negative word on *Smoldering Lust* begins to rumble through the network—and Burbank.

CHAPTER FIFTEEN
A MILE IN KATE'S SHOES

It's past midnight, and Gregg Barbanell, looking silly in shorts and women's dress shoes, is intently watching episode two of *Smoldering Lust.* The show is playing on a thirty-six-inch monitor at EFX. A digital readout in the lower left-hand corner of the monitor is ticking away each tenth of a second of videotape. When the clock hits 12:23:42, Gregg starts walking in place, delicately, on a concrete slab: click, click, click, pause; turn; scrape; click, click, click. Each of his footfalls is timed with Kate's on the screen as she makes her way in heels across a parking garage.

Pointing down at the floor, at Gregg's feet, picking up every click and scrape, is the slender rod of a powerful directional microphone. Gregg and his partner, Vince Nicastro, have been at it since nine this evening, filling in incidental sounds effects for the show, noises the boom mike didn't pick up during shooting. Footsteps, crumpling paper, rustling clothes, a telephone hanging up, a stylus gliding onto a scratchy old record—these may be among the most subtle sounds of *Smoldering Lust,* but without them the show would seem utterly artificial. Musicians by day, Gregg and Vince, by night, are what is known as foley artists.

The tricks they perform recall the early days of radio, when coconut shells were used to fake the clippity-clop of horses' hooves—the name *foley,* in fact, honors that golden age: Jack Foley was an early sound effects master. Foley artists are something of an elite; no more than fifty of them ply their trade around town, and they tend to keep vampire hours, sundown to sunrise, when the studios are empty. Tonight at EFX, after Bradley has completed a looping session and Jay and Leslie Dennis approved the computer-created squeaks for Hal's sneakers, Gregg and Vince take over the studio along with Brian Geer, who will mix the results in the control room.

Gregg, Vince, and Brian work on each show in three cycles, on three sound tracks: the first layer adds the rustle of clothing; then come footsteps, then all incidental sounds. Clutching an old cotton shirt in his lap as he sits cross-legged on the floor before the television screen, Gregg rubs the fabric together to match the visual action: quick little buffs as Chris takes off his stained dinner jacket; a harder, angrier SLAP-RUB as Margo wipes it down; some slow and gentle caressing as Brodsky brushes up against Eve's slinky cocktail dress. Isolated in the vaultlike atmosphere of the studio, the rustling of the shirt is an exaggerated, unfamiliar sound, but it will be nearly lost in the final product: if it's not, the foley artists have failed. Good foleying, unless it's done to create a special sound effect such as flesh being torn or slapped, should be virtually unnoticed.

Tiptoeing, barely breathing around the mike, Gregg and Vince stifle laughter and sometimes amazement at the shows, which they're watching for the first time. Occasionally Brian stops the tape to let out a pent-up giggle or sigh. "Who *is* that woman?" Gregg asks during the first break.

"Kate Capshaw," Brian reports, speaking through the intercom.

"Wow."

"Who's the girl?" asks Vince.

"Someone new," comes the answer from the control room. "Alison Elliott."

"Wow, too."

The foley stage is a foam-lined alcove at one end of the studio, padded cell-like, with several portable floor surfaces to work on, each about a yard square: wood, concrete, dirt, carpet. There's also a small sandpit to trudge through. Constantly changing shoes—all kinds are lying around, including sneakers, desert boots, leather-soled loafers, sandals, fuzzy bedroom slippers, and cowboy boots—Gregg and Vince mimic every footstep in *Smoldering Lust,* whether Chris's nervous slinking down the hotel corridor, Eve's meandering across the pine-planked photo studio, Brodsky's brisk shuffle up the concrete steps from his basement-level shop, or Margo's restless pacing across bathroom tiles. It's hard work, looking and listening so intently—watching with your ears, really, to synchronize your own body movements, even a slight turn of an ankle, to those of the characters on screen.

"Until you've foleyed, you don't realize how many different ways people might walk or run in a half-hour show," says Vince, who, like all foley artists, appreciates the finer points of particular actors' walks. As Margo, Kate often moves slowly, deliberately, as if thinking about each step; Alison starts and stops, a bit self-consciously, aware that men enjoy looking at Eve. Bradley's quick, loose-limbed Brodsky is an athletic challenge—"he's hard to keep up with," says the wiry Vince, who stands slightly inclined toward the screen as he works, hands behind his back, like a skater at a starting line. A half-hour show's worth of foley-walking can feel like a mile.

From the foley point of view, the situations in *Smoldering Lust* are routine. There are the usual office sounds to make, a little street noise, and the normal plunks, plops, slams, crunches, creaks, and pops of a household. This show is in fact easier to foley than most since the budget doesn't allow the Codys a kitchen, sparing Gregg and Vince the chores of filling in the whirs and beeps of appliances. There's no on-screen violence, either, which would have the foley guys tearing apart vegetables, sharpening knives, or slapping raw meat in front of the microphone. But they do get plenty of use out of the enormous inventory of flea market and garage sale finds that are the staples of the foley trade: throw pillows, rubber gloves, metal lunch boxes, a roll of hurricane fencing, a portable TV set, a Samsonite suitcase, milk cartons, a box of Cheerios, lamps and light switches, a shopping cart, teapots, a dustpan, doorknobs, and latches. There's even a sofa with rusty springs. "Some shows," says Brian, "you're shoving and dragging heavy furniture around all night, just to get the right bumps and grinds and whomps."

Though the inventory seems complete, when a scene comes up in which Margo punches Eve's number on a telephone, Gregg realizes they don't have a sufficiently late-model unit to match the sounds made by the one on the screen, so he dashes into the control booth to borrow one of the studio's phones. When Brian replays the scene for Gregg, his button-pushing is in sync with Kate's.

By three in the morning they're wrapping up the last of the third show. "Okay, guys," Brian says from the control room, "we missed something back there—those people wandering around Brodsky's record shop." Keeping close watch on his own monitor at the console, Brian backs up Gregg and Vince, spotting gaps they might miss. "Can you walk a little in there for me?" he asks.

"Sure," Vince answers. Then, to Gregg: "You want to be the woman?"

"Yeah, okay. She's wearing heels, right?" Gregg steps into a pair of leather-soled pumps, which will do for the well-dressed extra browsing in Brodsky's shop. The other actor, a man, is in sneakers, so Vince can stay in his Converse high-tops. First he, then Gregg, goes through the motions on the wooden floor square, perfectly in step with the action on the screen.

Completing the first three episodes, the pair are looking forward to the next batch. "I wish everything we worked on was this good," says Vince, who along with Gregg didn't bother to ask Brian which show they'd be foleying tonight. The credits aren't yet in place, so they don't even know what the title is or the names of the writers and producers. "Who did this show?" asks Gregg, tying his shoes. Brian, shutting down the high-tech end of the operation for the night, tells him.

"I knew it seemed familiar," says Gregg. "I did the foleying on *Molly Dodd* and *Buffalo Bill.* Same kind of jobs—basic background noise. Nothing to distract from the writing."

CHAPTER SIXTEEN
BEING THE CODY MAN

Reporting to Empire Studios, John Calvin could be one of Dorothy's gang arriving inside the gates of the Emerald City. Diane and Paula clip and groom him, buff his nails, pluck an unruly strand of eyebrow, pat on the pancake. Lani takes measurements and dashes off to assemble Chris Cody's casual but expensive wardrobe. The actor sits for portraits of the urban outdoorsman. Standing six-three, taller in cowboy boots and hat, and hollering big howdys on the set, John is someone who stands out at Empire, and that's the way he feels it ought to be. "I'm the Cody Man," he says. Making an effort to leave behind the self-doubt that about wore him down during the audition process, he glad-hands his way around the studio, greeting people by name (having at home, memorized the crew list). John makes it a point to leave his dressing room door open. "Good morning!" he calls as Kate shuffles down the hall to makeup. To his stand-in, a rail of a young man named Bill Bosacker, he gives a Stetson. "Thought you ought to have a hat like Cody's," the actor said when he presented it. "Now you're really part of the family." It's not yet eight this particular June morning, but John has already had a chipper discussion about the craft of acting with Judy Applegate, an eighteen-year-old extra who is as starry-eyed as they come in this business. She thinks John is terrific. "This is only my second day here," says Judy, whose job is to cross in front of the camera occasionally, busying herself as an employee of Cody Canyon. "Already John has taught me so much."

Clearly, John takes this Cody Man thing seriously, even dressing like the character off camera in crisp jeans, flannel shirts, vests, western-style boots and hat. "What's left for me to do?" Lani teases. "We should give you a wardrobe credit." He draws a parallel between Chris Cody's position at Cody Canyon and his own at the studio. "As the Cody Man," he says, "I'm the axis for the show. It's important that I set the pace and always be in an upbeat mood." But just as Chris Cody doesn't really run the family business (Margo does), John, despite the billing, is less a leading player than Bradley. As for clicking with Kate, this seems not to be, as Lori Oppenden so wanted, a Sam-and-Diane match. Kate could weep, the chemistry feels so wrong. And yet— wouldn't a lack of sparks, a forced show of affection, suit a portrayal of a yawning marriage? Sam and Diane they're not, but Kate and John do eventually hit their stride as a husband and wife who have (comically) lost the ability to communicate with one another.

John has the disadvantage of playing someone who does the unadmirable thing of fleeing a murder scene and who is incapable of shooting straight with anyone—wife, friends, colleagues, mistress. Chris Cody is not the towering redwood John seems to think he is. And yet, John learns how to make the character a lovable goofus. The actor's timing, his comic stupors, crack up the crew. Approaching Eve, who has casually dropped her bra in the Cody Canyon photo studio, Chris tries to avert his eyes, torn between loyalty to Margo and desire for Eve. Practically sprouting antlers right there, he knows he'll have to settle for rubbing against a tree. "I admire Margo so much," says the unclothed Eve, unself-consciously turning towards him. "She could teach me tons—do you think she'd take me under her wing?" Dry-mouthed, Cody softly replies: "Yes—I think she'd take you under her wing and crush you to death."

Again the crew is a good audience. John is not at ease with the subtlety of the material, and he hates playing comedy in the deep-freeze silence of the stage when the camera is rolling. Whenever there's time he runs through scenes with the crew around. "I like an audience," he says. "I know the lines so well I don't know if I'm being funny or not, so it's good to get some real laughs before we have to call quiet on the set."

After the dressing-room scene, Alison and John wander over to the catering table. Ignoring the junk food, she digs into the cooler for a bottle of juice. He pours coffee. "I heard you were in the navy in 1968," Alison says to him, amazement in her voice. "You know, I wasn't even born yet. And we're supposed to be lovers."

"That," John explains to her, "is one of the show's plot points."

When he's not in front of the camera, John busies himself around the set, making small talk, asking questions. "I intrude," he admits, asking Steve Confer about different film stock, Gillian Childers about the power of the boom mike, Ann about the floor plan for the Codys' cabin, Liz Matthews about her location search for the exterior of the Codys' house. "I want to learn about the nuts and bolts of my business. The more I know, the better for the show." Whether he gets answers or not, John believes it's important to hang around the set. "Anything to keep me thinking about the show. If you wander off or go back to your dressing room, you start thinking about other things. This way I feel like a producer, doing what I can to make the show go right."

Though well liked around the studio, John will never get close to Jay, who keeps him at arm's length, rarely inviting conversation outside the context of the production, and the actor can't help but feel excluded by the sociable triumvirate of Jay, Kate, and Bradley. John takes comfort in knowing that he's good in the role—he's getting good reports back from dailies, which show the convincingly estranged Margo and Chris—but it's increasingly apparent that Bradley is getting the best lines, and more of them, as Brodsky's opening and closing monologues become more important, his relationship with Margo deepens, and his time in front of the camera lengthens. A TV *Guide* squib makes it clear, describing the forthcoming series as a "deliciously titled comedy revolving around a San Francisco private detective." Take that, Cody Man.

CHAPTER SEVENTEEN
THE PROBLEM WITH PHILIP

"What," asks a fragile, morning-after Margo, "is wrong with men?" She's in her office, seeking comfort from her business manager, the snappy Philip Wingate. His shirt is crisply starched, tie perfectly knotted, and his reply doesn't miss a beat: "What's wrong with men? Have you got a few hours? And that's just for the table of contents." It may sound like another notch is being marked in the bedpost count of prime-time gay characters—a short but slowly growing list that began in 1970, when Hal Holbrook and Martin Sheen played lovers in the TV movie *That Certain Summer,* and continues with Sandra Bernhard's and Martin Mull's turns in *Roseanne*—but Philip Wingate, who makes his debut in the second episode of *Smoldering Lust,* doesn't really belong in that company. Philip is something of a throwback to stereotypes that have long dominated film and television portrayals of homosexuals and were chronicled by the late Vito Russo in his landmark study, *The Celluloid Closet.*

On the big and small screens, homosexual men and women are rarely trusting or trustworthy, loving or lovable. As the lone gay character in *Smoldering Lust,* Philip preys on the boss's fears and insecurities about men, is forever hissing at Eve, his rival for Margo's friendship, is even suspected of embezzling from Cody Canyon. Surely a challenging, multidimensional gay character could have been introduced in a series that so boldly addresses marital infidelity and (hetero)sexual passion, especially from the hand of Jay Tarses, who proved with *Slap Maxwell* that he had adventurous ideas on the subject (the series created one powerful cameo in a scene about a basketball coach who roughs up Dabney Coleman for confronting him with rumors of his homosexuality). But early outlines for the characters in *Smoldering Lust* reveal an unwillingness even to acknowledge Philip's sexuality, disingenuously describing him as "*not* gay, but not sad, either." Philip is not gay, but eager to dish men with Margo?

The fact that the character he plays is devious and closeted doesn't rile actor Patrick Bristow. Though as an openly gay actor he does have problems with Philip, he has much bigger ones with the idea of censorship in any form. "People like Philip do exist," he says while show three is being filmed. "The most important thing about him isn't his sexuality, anyway, but his absolute need to control everything and everyone around him. Especially Margo." Though not an attractive trait, Philip's control mania has nothing to do with his being gay or straight. The character is not a grossly offensive stereotype, one that GLAAD, the Gay and Lesbian Alliance Against Defamation, is likely to condemn. And, as Patrick says, if Philip is less than a positive role model, so are the other characters: "Philip is no more screwed up than anyone else around him—Eve, Margo, Brodsky, Chris, Hal." As for the character's sexual ambiguity, Patrick hopes people will be patient with him. "For now, I prefer to believe that he's a virgin. Philip could develop in surprising ways. Audiences will just have to give him time."

In his outline for show four, Russ stabs at rehabilitating Philip, noting that the character "is not just a nasty eavesdropping troublemaker—he and Margo have a very genuine friendship." The bond between Margo and Philip is indeed crucial to the success of the series; it is, after all, his idea that she hire a private investigator to trail Chris, which is the defining action of the story. Kate looks forward to her scenes with Patrick, which could, she imagines, illustrate the relationships that can develop between straight women and gay men. But when she and Patrick take their places on the Cody Canyon set to run through their first scene together, she doesn't feel the connection between the two characters. Shot out of sequence, the scene is from the third episode. After the first early-morning read-through, then another, Kate seems bothered, voicing her displeasure with the character rather than the person playing him. "This is supposed to be my best friend?" she asks. "This is the person I most trust?" No one ventures an answer, and the tension hangs in the air for a moment. Patrick can only pretend not to hear.

Recuperating from the awful moment, the actor charges back into the scene. It begins deliciously, with Margo's office invaded by a group of high school students who have come to Cody Canyon on a field trip to learn about the business world (already a joke, since the bosses seem so scatterbrained). Philip is late to the office today, so Margo must conduct the tour. Among the students is an earnest know-it-all named Heidi who has an annoying knack for asking questions that unintentionally hit sore spots: "Do you have any children? If not, why not?" Then: "What's it like working with your husband? Please be specific." As the stage directions have it, "Margo would rather leap out the window than face this," and she is hugely relieved to spot Philip darting past her door.

"Where have you been?" she cries. Poking his head into her office, he apologizes for oversleeping. Margo grills him right there in front of the youngsters: "In eight years you've never been late once. Why didn't you call?"

"I couldn't call when I was sleeping, could I, angel?"

"If you overslept, then why was your car here when I got in?"

Philip ends the embarrassing exchange by offering to take over the tour, adding, "I don't think Mom and Dad should fight in front of the children."

Philip eventually returns to Margo's office with a peace offering, a plate of sweets. "You know I can't be around things like that," she says, but as Philip fills her in on more upsetting details about Chris's dalliance with Eve, she grabs a sugary piece of Danish. Philip looks pleased.

Patrick attributes the bumpy beginning with Kate to something like opening-night jitters and trusts that they will grow more comfortable with one another. "Except for the run-throughs," he says, "we have no rehearsal time. There's no discussion with anyone writing or directing the show about Margo and Philip, about who our characters are, why we're supposedly so attached to one another. All of which would be fine if the scenes were working for us. But they're not yet, and it's easy for an actor to feel orphaned. I'm missing the enthusiasm that was shown when I got the job."

A quick wit whose performing career began in the foxholes of improvisational comedy, Patrick is fearless onstage without a script. The quiet ensemble work of *Smoldering Lust* is something new, and he hankers for the fast pace of skits and immediate audience reactions. Cheryl Bayer knew of Patrick from his work with the Groundlings, the Hollywood comedy troupe that has nurtured such talents as Julia Sweeney of *Saturday Night Live*. A regular at the company's theater on Melrose Avenue, Patrick was known for his portrayals of a terrorist Irish poet, of Queen Elizabeth I, and of Jane Hathaway, the prim secretary played by Nancy Kulp on *The Beverly Hillbillies*.

Casting the pilot for a comedy revue for Carsey-Werner productions, Cheryl invited Patrick to her office. The show never got off the ground, but Cheryl, who was dazzled by Patrick, knew she'd made a find. When *Smoldering Lust* came along she thought of him first thing for the role of Philip. Though she also tried out other actors for the part, Patrick was the one she urged on the producers. "He's fresh, a new face," she told them. "There's nothing generic about him. In this show particularly, where each character has a signature, he'd be perfect."

Returning to Cheryl's office in Studio City to read for Philip, Patrick was anxious. He had just completed a short run as an eighty-six-year-old codger on a children's television program and planned to be off to Seattle and San Francisco soon to don a rabbit costume for a department store promotion. The only other gig on his schedule was a trade show, where he was to do the offstage voice of a menacing computer, so he wasn't exactly casual about this shot at network television. Nor was his agent, Scott Manners, who signed Patrick after seeing him at the Groundlings. Scott too immediately thought of him when the breakdown sheet describing the character of Philip Wingate arrived: "in his late 20s to early 30s ... Always upbeat and encouraging and a clear-thinker ... fastidious, efficient, ambitious ... " The role, Scott thought, might be a bit confining for such a gifted comic actor as Patrick, but he had no hesitation about telling his client to go for it; the part would be "a hell of a network debut."

At the reading in her office, Cheryl put Patrick at ease. She couldn't say much about the show since only three scripts had been finished, but she assured him that *Smoldering Lust* wouldn't be ordinary television. "You can take this character a long way," she told him as they began reading a scene together. The first line was Patrick's: "Margo, my dove, you look ashen and wan"— and off they went through the three pages of dialogue. Cheryl coached Patrick, telling him to try again, this time with less sarcasm. "Philip's really concerned about Margo here," she said. They took it again. "Good," said Cheryl, "but sweeten it just a little more. Philip's the one person who's taking care of Margo, and that feeling should come through." On the third go Patrick's "ashen and wan" was uttered as Cheryl thought it ought to be, less as criticism than as concern. "Lovely," Cheryl told him. As far as she was concerned, he had the part. That night, at home in his cottage in Silver Lake, Patrick cautiously started to think the same thing.

Summoned next to Empire to read for the producing team, he was confident—so much so that he felt no twinges as he nodded at the half-dozen or so other actors gathered there, clutching script pages to their chests. Because of his socko session with Cheryl, he allowed himself the pleasure of thinking that the audition at the studio was a formality and the fact that he was the last to be called into Elaine Avata's office seemed to bear that out; they were saving the best for last, surely.

Reading for the small but important audience gathered in Elaine's office, Patrick began with Philip's observation that Margo is "ashen and wan."

Cheryl, again as Margo: "We slept in separate rooms last night."

PHILIP

Ah well, at least you slept.

MARGO

No, I didn't, Philip. Not a wink. Look at my eyes.

PHILIP

Timeless beauty is all I see. Care-worn maybe... but elegant and everlasting, nonetheless.

MARGO

You're a pal, Philip. Through thick and thin. I can always count on you. Well... we'd better get to work.

PHILIP

Yes, let's. Lots to do today.

MARGO

I *can't* work. I can't function with this guillotine on my back.

PHILIP

Monkey.

MARGO

What?

PHILIP

A guillotine would have to go over your head. A monkey would be on your back.

MARGO

Right. Sorry.

About the wisdom of hiring a private detective, Philip assures Margo that the strategy is "aggressive, forceful, and bold. It represents everything you are as a woman of the nineties. I'm proud to be associated with such a lioness." The scene ends with Margo telling Philip, "You're a dear friend and a trusted collaborator ... With no ulterior motive or personal agenda that I can see." Philip replies, "None whatsoever."

Jay and Rick were delighted with Patrick's sassy delivery. *Smoldering Lust* is not a show written for big laughs, but a few greeted the malapropism about guillotines and monkeys and Patrick's use of exaggerated hand gestures to clarify his meaning. Roundly thanked as he took his leave, Patrick heard a murmur that sounded like "terrific ... he gets it ... " He floated home.

The next day Scott called his client with the mostly great news: Patrick had the part, but it's being called a guest role, not a regular one, which put enormous pressure on the actor to get it right from the very beginning. "If Philip's not working out," he says at the beginning of production, "they'll kill him off or send him packing and get Margo a new assistant." But after the third episode is filmed, Patrick is essentially promoted from guest to regular player. He begins to relax a little, to let loose, bringing to the set some of the spontaneity he exercises so easily on the stage.

When Patrick signed on for the role, he did so knowing only as much about Philip as he could glean from the audition scenes and from that coy notation about the character being *"not gay, but not sad, either."* If the character were purely villainous, Patrick would have reason to register complaints with the writers. "Philip actually has a lot going for him," he says. "He's smart, and I choose to believe he's loyal. He loves Margo, and he's mean to Eve only because she threatens that primary relationship. And if he's doing something at the office on the sly, it's to spare Margo bad news about the company."

Prime-time gay bashing isn't always blatant. More often it takes a benign form, as in that which mars an early and still frequently broadcast episode of *Cheers.* That's the show in which a former baseball teammate of Sam Malone's comes out of the closet. Sam wrestles with the issue until deciding to stick by his buddy, telling him, "Hey—you didn't desert me when I had a drinking problem." There it is: homosexuality as a problem or sickness, like alcoholism. *Smoldering Lust* doesn't improve much on this state of affairs, though its makers, like those of *Cheers,* surely mean well. The Codys' political correctness embraces gay rights (although specific words to that effect, in show nine, Leslie Dennis is forced to edit out for time). When Chris fumbles around trying to explain to Eve why they should call off their flirtations, she interrupts him by asking, "Is this the gay confession?" Alison's throwaway delivery signals no alarm about a possible yes answer. Russ's outline notes for episode five, when Cody and Brodsky find themselves alone together in the Codys' cabin, explore the possibilities, more to deepen character than to get laughs: "Here in Cody's unused love nest (the motel room) Brodsky and Cody are men in heat. Brodsky is inflamed with passion for Margo … and Cody is about to explode from the frustration of his passion for Eve. These two men like each other. And while they don't dance, if the lights were different and the right song were playing and a bottle of cold champagne were nearby, well, it wouldn't be out of the question." At another point in the same outline, sketching out a scene where Margo confronts Eve about her interest in Cody, Russ notes that "Eve is finishing her modeling assignment for the day ... Margo is watching. We don't know whether Margo is afflicted with, well, smoldering lust for Eve, or whether Eve is making her think of Cody and how Margo herself used to be. In any event, she leaves a note that Eve should join her in her office."

But the writers' good intentions and flashes of worldimess in the show do not entirely conquer the problem they've created with Philip.

CHAPTER EIGHTEEN
TESTY

On the first of October, about six hundred households scattered throughout the top twenty markets tune in to a normally scrambled cable channel. NBC's research department has telephoned, asking them to help out by watching two episodes of *Smoldering Lust.* Most of the respondents are already familiar with the drill—the network conducts about a hundred such surveys every year—and know they'll be called back in a day or two and asked their opinions about the show. Did they like the story? How would they classify the program—comedy? drama? Which characters did they like best? Then the really big ones: Would they watch the show on a regular basis? If so, when? Mondays at nine, Saturdays at ten? It's a lot to ask of working people, and there's a bit of money to be made by those who take the time to watch and then submit to the quizzing. The identities of the cable-test households, like those of the Nielsen families, are a closely guarded secret. All the network will admit to is that the sample is representative of the country at large in the diversity of its demographics and, more important, in buying habits.

Smoldering Lust, which doesn't strive to be straightforward in the way that sitcoms usually are and whose story line inches along deliberately, may be a particularly difficult show to sample out of sequence, but NBC insists on pairing the first episode with a later one in order to give viewers, so the thinking goes, a "panorama" of action and characters. It is thus that on that autumn night the first and eleventh episodes of *Smoldering Lust* were screened back to back. In the first show, Chris Cody discovers the dead body in Room 1216 and Dave Brodsky walks the audience through the muddle of the Codys' marriage and the murder mystery. Much the same things seem to be going on in number eleven, with the marriage bumbling along and Brodsky halfheartedly poking through the evidence of sin and crime.

"They'll test the show to death, and the results will be dismal," says Jay. "They spend hundreds of thousands of dollars every year trying to find out who or what a target audience is. That might work for some kinds of shows, but not mine. With my work, the questions seem designed for failure. It used to be, 'Do you like the character of Buffalo Bill?' The answer has to be no—you're not supposed to like him. But negative answers lower the score. So there's no way that testing can be good for *Smoldering Lust.* NBC says they know that, that they're gonna ignore the test results and go ahead and market the show the way they want to anyway."

The show does test badly, and the news is trumpeted in a report sent around to the network's key department heads, including Eric Cardinal, the chief of research. "Viewers disliked all three lead characters," the report states, "and the remainder of the cast demonstrated little appeal." Brodsky is found to be "goofy," and "a nerd" whose "verbose narration is intrusive and distracting." Chris comes across as "too bumbling and inept to be a company president … phony, cold … superficial." Margo's "neurotic indecisiveness and fickle behavior," the scalding report continues, are "off-putting."

As for the show itself, viewers found it "sexually suggestive and tasteless" (compared to what—*Married with Children*?), "suspenseless" and "not entertaining or particularly funny." The story line is criticized for being hard to follow (which it would be, with a ten-show gap between episodes, though this mollifying factor is not mentioned in the report). The final grade on the show's overall performance: "Weak."

NBC, after committing millions of dollars to make *Smoldering Lust,* spends an additional $50,000 to conduct the test and circulate in-house the resulting report card, which contains not a single good word—not even for the music, production design, or any of the performances. The two-page, singlespaced report is the first most network departments hear of the show, the final episodes of which are still in postproduction, being edited, sound-mixed, and color-corrected. And it may be all they ever hear. To those inside NBC's advertising sales, programming, and promotion department, *Smoldering Lust* might as well have a big red flag on it that says ROTTEN GOODS or KICK ME.

For the truth is, the network will use the test to destroy the show. Citing the poor results, and the gloating summary of them, programming and other department heads can set the show aside, relegating it to the bottom of their priority lists. Doing so they will ignore the network's own valuable experience and lessons to the contrary. "If you can't really tag a show," says Brandon Tartikoff, "can't tell people what it is, the test results are always going to be awful. *Cheers* didn't test well—a show about people hanging out in a bar all day? The first handful of people who saw it didn't get it. *St. Elsewhere* also flunked, and if we had listened to the reports on *Miami Vice* we never would have cast Don Johnson."

To a quantifier like Eric Cardinal, charged with overseeing, interpreting, and disseminating the network's audience surveys, television shows are a product, actors are measurable production elements, audiences are targets, and writers and producers are trouble. It is his mission to assign numerical values to the experience of being entertained; one program thus might rate a seven on one scale, an actor score a three on another, a character soar to the top of yet another measuring stick. Eric is aware of the hazards of this practice—that data may be skewed, that analysis is necessarily subjective—but says that network executives do read between the lines (or the columns) of the surveys. Surrounded by multiple editions of *Performer Q, TV Q,* and other high-density marketing bibles that rate actors and their work on demographic appeal, he defends the testing process. "We ask respondents a lot about the general attributes of a program. We want to know if people think something is humorous, contemporary, thought-provoking, emotionally involving. When scores come up positive for a show, an actor, or a character, we try to find out if it's something they really like or just think they should like." He is talking about the social desirability bias, which comes up all the time in research. "The response to a show like *I'll Fly Away* may be motivated by the feeling that the show is good medicine, something you *should* watch. We have to be careful of that, because what we're selling is entertainment. That's where we put the most value—not on what people feel a duty about, but on where and how and why people seek out entertainment."

Stating the obvious, that "characters are very important to series television," Eric is speaking comparatively: compared to the story. "We find that if people warm up to a character," he says, "they'll come back to the show. If they don't like the characters then we've lost them, even if they like the story." That's why the popularity-contest rankings in *Performer Q* are important to him, and why he is concerned about the character bashing in the report on *Smoldering Lust.* "It wouldn't matter if the creative departments were high on the show. If the show has supporters here, then no scores are too low, no character too unlikable. We can always be overruled, and thank God for that—it's all about sticking up for what you think has value. It happened with *Grand,* which had terrible research—but some of the development people believed in it, and they got the programming department to put it on after *Cheers.* After a strong beginning the show faltered, and if the research had been promising we could've stepped in and said, Let's give it another chance, it tested okay. But it didn't, and when the ratings dipped, the development people had had their chance, and we had to let it go."

However much he may respect his colleagues in development, Eric hates it when they make blind commitments, such as the extraordinary concession to Jay to film thirteen episodes at once, especially since none were to air during production and no audience surveys would be available to shape the making of the show. The testing for *Smoldering Lust* occurs after the fact: show thirteen is being scored when shows one and eleven are sent up the flagpole. "The problem with this project is that Jay was allowed to just go off and write," says Eric, who would have welcomed the chance to weigh in with some of his data. "We could have pinpointed the show's strengths and weaknesses and come up with some ideas for improving audience appeal."

Though as a twenty-something-year veteran of commercial television he should know better, Jay claims that the notion of aiming for the widest possible audience appeal makes his blood "run cold." No one, least of all an MBA or a lawyer or a statistician, is going to tell him how to write. His talk is tough. "People who run the business side of this aren't show people or artists anymore, and so we've begun to work at cross-purposes. I find all this reliance on testing terrifying because the networks really do go by it and because those of us considered talent can be controlled by it."

It's not unusual for a network to spend $50 million a year to market-research its new programs, a fact that deepens the blotches of red in Bernie Brillstein's St. Nicholas cheeks. "It happens all the time," he says. "You're bravely signed up to do a show. Then they test it and lose their nerve. But since eighty percent of all new shows fail, the research obviously isn't telling the networks what they need to know. I doubt if the ratio of success is even ten percent. You can go crazy doing the arithmetic on the fifty million they waste on research: for that amount of money I could put on eight shows with the best people in the business. If they're determined to research something, then why not research the research? I'd be a much poorer man if I listened to my test results. The word in 1976 on *The Muppet Show* was that you can't have a frog host a show, so don't do it. Before that, when I put *Hee-Haw* together, everyone laughed and started waving audience predictions at me. And our first night on the air we got a forty-one share. We stayed on for twenty-three years. Same story with *Saturday Night Live* almost twenty years ago—no one wanted to give us seventeen weeks because the research indicated it would be a one-shot success."

Since filming of all thirteen episodes of *Smoldering Lust* is complete by the time the tests are done, the only question left for Eric is scheduling. "One of the most important things we ask is how much of an effort people would make to watch the show. Would they plan an evening around it? That gets us thinking specifically about when to air the show." And that brings Eric to Preston Beckman, the man at NBC who gets first crack at the programming board, the Sunday-through-Saturday grid of time slots that resembles a train station's departure board. Responsible for filling twenty-one hours of prime time, three hours a night, seven days a week, Preston says he is guided by one consideration: "to get the biggest audience I can for a show, whether it's good or bad—I don't care." But rather than boldly attempting to target a particular show for the big numbers, meaning the sizable audience of viewers between eighteen and forty-nine that advertisers dream about, he does the reverse, delivering the numbers to the show. Even if he were fond of *Smoldering Lust,* no network program director would think of filling the yummy spots on the grid with such fare. As Preston bluntly puts it, "What's given the best chance to succeed may not be the best show."

With his reddish beard, glasses, and V-neck sweaters, he has a professional look about him, and in fact he does hold a doctorate in sociology, which he taught before leaving academia for television. The discipline, he says, comes in handy at the network, though not to help him better understand and analyze television audiences and their viewing habits; rather, his background "helps me deal with the people in this company."

Before the show is tested, Preston saw only the first four episodes of *Smoldering Lust,* and he resents having to deal with the series. "We never should have made it," he says. "I suppose we have to honor our relationships with certain people, but we shouldn't even have this show around to worry about. It won't work. Look at what the hell's working: things that make you feel good, that bring you into a family. This show doesn't do that, and you can't compare it to *Seinfeld,* which is obvious, out-there comedy. This is a business of familiarity; people don't like to be challenged a lot. What the hell is *Smoldering Lust?*"

For NBC he fears it's another "walk on the dark side" in the manner of *Homicide, Law and Order, I'll Fly Away,* and *Northern Exposure.* His point is that those shows, while successful, take viewers places they don't necessarily want to be—a tiny town in Alaska, gritty Baltimore, the South before the civil rights movement, an impoverished Caribbean island—and he is reluctant to push his luck by adding the moody San Francisco of *Smoldering Lust* to that list. "This one won't work," he says. "Who would want to spend time in the world Jay has created? It's not a happy, hopeful place. It's a narrow, narrow show. If it appeals to anyone, it'll be women aged nineteen to thirty-four. Men don't turn to network television for sex; they've got the Playboy Channel, so that's not a market for this show." He adds that teens won't get it either, not like they get *Blossom.* "That's turned out to be a place we can have a little sex," says Preston. "The show was already doing fine, and then Susan Anton appeared in one episode. The overnight numbers went way up, a real jump, and it was all because of teenage boys. So I went down to development with one word of advice for the future of the show: 'Tits.' That's what I said to them: 'Tits.' "

If he had his way, Preston would edit *Smoldering Lust* into one-hour episodes—not because the stories would play better at that length, but "just to get rid of them quicker." His next-best strategy is to wait for summer. "We should sneak it in when nothing else is going on. At least we'll get press then. The idiots, they'll probably write about the show in a positive way, call it smart or sophisticated or sexy. So we won't get beat up there. Then we'll be done with it." He mentions Saturdays at nine-thirty or ten, and though twenty years have passed since *The Mary Tyler Moore Show* made it fashionable for young adults stay home and watch TV on that weekend night, it is a familiar place for comedy on NBC, with *Mad About You* and *Empty Nest* for neighbors. At the suggestion that *Smoldering Lust* be positioned behind *Seinfeld*, like a football placed for kickoff, Preston says never, perhaps ending right there any chance the show might have of finding the kind of audience that would most appreciate it. But who at NBC can afford to do a show such a favor? "If you're number one," says Preston, "you can experiment with your winners. This network is in no position to carry any excess baggage right now. We're losing every race."

The scheduling decision doesn't have to be made for a while, but when it's time Preston will consult the test report, which so caustically confirms what he already thinks about the series. There are times, Preston says, when he wants to damn test scores and fight for the series, actors, too. But not this series. When *Smoldering Lust* sinks—when, he says, not if—he knows that the network will be vilified by the writers, producers, critics, even the actors. "Actors," Preston says. "You do everything for them, support their shows, and when they finally get into a position of power they start in, saying the network is the cause of all their problems. They forget what we've done for them, how we've stuck by them. You know, if we hadn't stuck with *Cheers,* who would Ted Danson be?

CHAPTER NINETEEN
PHOTO OP

"I am dreading it. *Dreading* it," says Lani, pins in her mouth. Bruce McGill, in his boxer shorts, is trying on a new suit for Hal, something in a brown plaid with big shoulders. "Hugo Boss?" he asks. Lani shakes her head. He wonders aloud if the shoulders are too broad, but Lani is too preoccupied to discuss the cut of Bruce's jacket. It's September 24—show thirteen is about to wrap—time for what's known as a gallery shoot, a glorified cast photograph staged by the network publicity department.

"In my experience they always insist on doing the most inappropriate things," says Lani, who has dressed dozens of gallery shoots for sitcoms, TV movies, and specials. "The photograph is supposed to represent a show. So what do the network people do? Misrepresent it. If you don't hover over them, they'll put the actors in the most ridiculous poses. Just watch—they'll try to put a smoking gun in Kate's hand. The murderous Margo: did she or didn't she do it? That may make an amusing picture on the TV page, but it's untrue to the show. I wouldn't be surprised if they ask John to lie down so Kate can put a foot on his chest. And no matter how many costumes I bring from the actors' wardrobes, they'll come up to me whining, 'Don't you have anything with more color?' And for the women, 'More revealing?' "

"What about me?" Bruce asks. He should be prepared for anything, Lani tells him; they might want him to twiddle his mustache like the villain in a melodrama.

A memo has gone around to all the actors announcing the photo call for Saturday. Alison drops by wardrobe to ask what she should expect. "Are they going to vamp me?" she asks. "Well, that's what this is all about," says Lani. "But if you don't like what they put you in or what they ask you to do, just tell them 'No—I'm not comfortable doing this.' If they persist, I'll stop them."

The photo session causes an upheaval in the show's shooting schedule, which is moved from Friday to the following Monday to give the actors time to rest up so that they will look their best for the photographers. "We can't keep them here late on Friday," Jay says to Lani. "Not with a gallery shoot the next morning." For wardrobe especially the gallery shoot is a complicated undertaking, like any location work—or as Lani prefers to call it, "a day camp, but in fancy dress." She and Lisa Wilson and Brenda Maben are in charge of packing up several changes of costumes.

By ten on Saturday morning the *Smoldering Lust* gang, supervised by Elaine Arata, converges with the network bunch led by NBC program publicist Bob Meyer, a polite, soft-spoken redhead from New Orleans. The site is a baroque villa in the exclusive enclave of San Marino. The grand house, built by the society architect Wallace Neff in the twenties, is on the market for $6.7 million; it's not selling, so the owners, who do not live here and have let a tangle of rosebushes take over the once prim gardens, hire it out to film and photo crews. The opulent place could serve a show like *Dynasty* nicely, but Lani and her colleagues have no idea why it was chosen for *Smoldering Lust*. The marble staircases and loggia are lovely, the Corinthian columns and crystal chandeliers gorgeous, but this is supposed to be the Codys' house? Margo and Chris would never live in such opulence. Uncomfortable, Alison asks, "What are we doing *here?* This is out of character."

Wardrobe takes over the library, wheeling in three racks of clothes and piling up hat and shoe boxes. Turning a bathroom into a makeshift hair and makeup room, Diane and Paula start on the actors, first putting Alison in curlers. Elaine, functioning as field-trip coordinator, trots back and forth between her people and the network's. Lani is grateful for her presence. "It's not the norm to have a producer at these things. Most producers can't be bothered, leaving us, and the actors, at the mercy of the stylists and photographers and publicists."

What the network is aiming for is articulated by Charlotte Simpson, whom NBC has hired to design print ads for the show. "What we want to convey," she says to the two freelance photographers assigned to the job, "is sex—but sex with a twist." The photographers, Chris Reisig and Leeza Taylor, do not ask her to explain. Brenda Hurst, another NBC hand, has made a list of the specific shots she wants: "John Calvin—evening clothes & outdoor gear; Alison Elliott—sexy; John and Kate together; John looking at Eve."

An hour passes, then another, as the photographers and their assistants prepare setups, place props, and check lights and the actors sashay from hair to makeup to wardrobe. The grumbling about the site fades and spirits are high; this isn't such a bad way to spend half a Saturday, especially for actors, being fussed over and indulging in some giddy talk about the show's prospects. Kate and Bradley, John and Alison all tell one another how smashing the show is. Dashing about with a clipboard, the network's Bob Meyer stokes the enthusiasm, saying that *Smoldering Lust* will surely fly if it gets a good time slot: "This show is too good for a lower shelf in the back of the store, though. It has to be prominently displayed, near the cash registers."

Getting down to business, he reminds the actors why they're here this morning, and it's not simply to sit for a pretty portrait: "These pictures have to sell that premiere episode, get those first-night numbers way up." He describes the ideal gallery shoot as "one that intrigues—something to make people tune in." A tireless cheerleader for the industry, Bob attributes his career choice, almost seriously, to watching reruns of *Bewitched* during his college days at Southern Methodist University, where he studied broadcasting. "That show to me was just an entertaining way to talk about prejudice," he says. "That was the whole premise—how people pass judgment on others who are different, how neighbors turn against each other."

As the hours pass in San Marino, it's obvious that Bob has done an unusual job with the *Smoldering Lust* shoot, neither humiliating the actors nor betraying the spirit of the show. Lani is amazed. Only once is an objection raised, by Alison, when she's asked to put on Eve's scanty cavewoman getup. The outfit is a deliberate joke, one of the crackpot concepts for the Cody Canyon catalog; out of context, though, it seems nothing but silly and sexist. When Alison demurs Bob says fine, deleting the shot from the list. The photographers' best picture is a group portrait of the four principals piled onto a sofa, their limbs intertwined, echoing a famous movie still from twenty years ago—Chris, Margo, Brodsky, and Eve as *Bob & Carol & Ted & Alice*. This is the picture that will be dispatched to the media, to run in TV columns and in Sunday magazines, and Bob thinks it's a winner. It will go out with a news release he is writing that strives to make a virtue of the difficulty the press will have in categorizing *Smoldering Lust*. "Start with a detective," the news release begins, "add one body and a philandering husband, throw in a suspicious wife and you've got—excuse me? Did someone say a situation comedy?" Back in his Burbank office Monday morning Bob privately worries that even with a terrific gallery shoot this show is going to be one hard sell.

CHAPTER TWENTY
KEEPING IT CLEAN

It's just before noon and Elaine's telephone rings for what she swears is the twenty-second time. Tom Posivak is calling, from NBC's department of standards and practices. He's got a problem with Brodsky's crude mouth again. The character starts off show eleven by admitting he'd like to bang Margo. "Can't you guys come up with something a little more delicate?" Tom asks. Elaine takes the matter up later in the day with Rick. "Brodsky talks like that," Rick tells her to tell Tom. It's true—Brodsky often does sound like a horny teenager; his idea of showing his sensitive side is to ask Cookie if she objects to "the demeaning and sexually explicit way I refer to women."

The word "bang" may suit the character, but it still bothers Tom. As always, he worries what affiliates and advertisers might do if they perceive the show as crossing the line of decency. He's not ordering the writers and producers to make a change, just strongly suggesting that they do. Easygoing and genuinely fond of the show, Tom has given it little grief, and Rick and Jay agree to accommodate him on this point. There's no time to argue, anyway; the scene will be shot in two days.

It'll be a location shoot, with Brodsky walking along a city street, rambling on about his unrequited lust for Margo. He stops in front of a small office building, noticing a name on the intercom. It's a psychiatrist's office (as if the doctor's specialty would be listed). He buzzes. The doctor doesn't have time to see him but agrees to do a quick session right there over the intercom. Lowering his voice, Brodsky starts in on what's happening with him and Margo, what's not happening, wonders what's wrong. "You could be experiencing sexual dysfunction," says the doctor loudly, causing three young women walking by to do a double take. Muffling the speaker with one hand, Brodsky says, "Doc, you've got it all wrong ... I didn't want to ... bang her." Reworking the exchange, Jay and Rick have the doctor finish Brodsky's sentence for him.

RICK: "Brodsky says, 'I only wanted to—' and the doctor cuts him off with, 'You wanted to—*putz* her.'"

JAY: "Can't say 'putz.'"

RICK: " 'You wanted to ... you wanted to ... show her in and out.'"

JAY: " 'You wanted, you wanted ... to slip her the bishop.'"

Slip her the bishop? Elaine faxes the new page over to Tom; she'd rather not convey the change over the telephone. He is gleeful, certain that few will even get the reference. "If you don't know chess," he says, "the phrase doesn't play. I'm betting that at least half the audience won't get the phallic reference."

All over Burbank there's grumbling about standards and practices: the censors, the taste police, the black-hooded destroyers of creativity. But standards and practices people aren't the Inquisition; they're just executives caught between writers and producers and the three A's: audiences, advertisers, and affiliates. It's the affiliates that take the heat when viewers are offended by program content. Tom, a thirty-year veteran of the network, tries to anticipate flare-ups in order to keep the local stations out of trouble. "That's where the roadblocks start," he says. "When viewers don't like what they see or hear on channel four, they don't call us first, they call their local station." Well organized and funded these days, viewer groups are exerting real influence over television programming, and Tom encourages such feedback on the issue of excessive violence on TV. But when it comes to the highly politicized debates about morality and so-called family values he is not so welcoming, viewing crusades to rein in creative writers and performers as dangerous. "There are people out there who obviously do not think television should deal with the realities of life. We do want to know what our viewers find too suggestive, and we'll work with them. But if organizations start dictating what gets on the air, we'd never do anything controversial, anything real. We'd never talk about adoption or abortion. *Cheers* never would've have happened—a show built around an alcoholic? People come up to me and say, 'Hey, you had a gay guy in a show last night.' Well, so what—we also had on a black couple and a woman in a wheelchair and an unwed working mother. We've got to put on shows that let people know we are dealing with reality." And that, he strongly believes, includes the marital minefield navigated in *Smoldering Lust.*

Protective of the affiliates, Tom also runs defense for writers. He tries to "leave a script as untouched as possible" as it makes its way from the writer's desk to broadcast. *Smoldering Lust* does not cause him the kind of headaches he has suffered over the provocative *L.A. Law,* though for a network comedy, the new show does start explosively: with a bloody corpse in a hotel room and all that furtive lovemaking. Tom would prefer that the writers not go quite so far on the first date. "At the beginning of a new series we like to bend over backward not to offend the affiliates and the audience," he says to Elaine after reading the first three scripts. "Can you guys hold back a little, until the audience is more familiar with the characters?" After talking with Jay, Elaine gets back to Tom: "Trust us. It'll be fine. You'll see in the dailies." Tom's heard that before from this team, on *Molly Dodd* and *Buffalo Bill,* and concedes that usually they're right. He agrees that the corpse scene may be shot as written, but after viewing dailies he resumes his argument, calling Leslie Dennis while she's editing the episode. "There's blood all over the place," he tells her. "I have to turn away. It looks like the girl was knifed. Haven't you got a long shot?" Leslie tries recutting, using a quick close-up of the body and then pulling back, keeping most of the scene in the shadows. She also dissolves quickly, obliging Tom's request to "get us out of there fast."

As for the flagged bedroom scene, it also remains as written. "I wish we could have a little more build-up to this moment," he says, watching the dailies in his bungalow office on the NBC lot. Margo, in something brief and sheer, is approaching Chris in bed. The camera peers into her cleavage, then scans Chris's bare chest. As Tom watches, he gets Elaine on the telephone. "This is wonderful," he tells her, "but I'd still be a lot more comfortable if I'd known these characters a little longer. Isn't this a lot to handle right off the bat?"

Elaine says, "They're married, Tom. It's a married couple. Margo and Chris Cody."

Tom says, "Right. And a few minutes ago he was about to jump into bed with a girl. But she was dead. Nice marriage." Tom is saying these things mostly as a matter of going on the record with his unease about the material; for now he is content to wait and see. As more episodes arrive on his desk, he is relieved to see that the whole of the show is less problematic than the individual parts. "The cumulative effect of the episodes takes care of just about everything that bothered me," he says. "Some of the individual scenes are very risqué, taking you right to the edge. Like the time where it looks like Margo and Brodsky are going to make love right there on his desk. But those dangerous moments dissolve, and the situations evolve into something else, something more meaningful.

"Because things aren't what they seem in *Smoldering Lust,* the writers get away with a lot. Each episode contains strong stuff, but if you take the show as a series—as a big, long movie—then you see it's not offending anyone. It's really a very gentle way of dealing with a controversial subject, adultery, and with each episode it goes a step further. You wonder how far it'll go."

The words of writers are sacrosanct to Tom, and he dislikes asking even for small changes in a text. "The most offensive thing I can imagine is not any profanity that might turn up in a script, but that I or anyone at the network would presume to do the writer's job. That just doesn't make any sense to me. If we've hired you to write a show, then why should we step in and tell you how to do it?" When Chris Cody, caught in a lie, blames some "bastard," Tom doesn't follow his request for another word with an alternative of his own. "I know how this kind of quibble must sound to a writer who has created characters with their own way of speaking," he says. "If I try to do it myself I'll come up with something like 'jerk,' and you'll wonder what planet I'm from." The trouble in this case is that the writers can't come up with anything else either. Elaine makes the plea: "If you don't like it in dailies, we'll loop in something else. But you'll see, it fits the moment." Again, watching the filmed scene play out, Tom agrees: in the silliness of the moment, uttered in desperation, the "bastard" is not offensive, not name-calling. It's just funny.

Tom winds up letting the often faithless, occasionally cussing characters of *Smoldering Lust* do and say just about anything the writers want them to. "The show is laughing at lust," he says, which makes it difficult for him to do much serious slashing with his red pencil. "I've come a long way from my *Dragnet* debacle," he says, referring to a long-ago crisis when he allowed Sergeant Joe Friday to say "go to hell" on the popular police show. The outcry from the affiliates was wild, as if NBC had smashed the Ten Commandments. People wanted to wash Sergeant Friday's mouth out with soap. "He never said it again," says Tom.

By the time he's completed his work on the series, Tom is bothered by just one thing, both as censor and viewer. "It's that poor girl in Room 1216," he says. He dislikes the fact "that somewhere along the way, interest in solving the crime dwindles and no one gives a damn. Everyone's forgotten about her." A murder's been committed and all anyone cares about is getting laid. But that's the writers' business, not his. The problem, Tom figures, will take care of itself: if viewers don't like it they'll either holler at their affiliates, or switch channels.

CHAPTER TWENTY-ONE
NIT-PICKING

After shooting commences, any errors or legal problems with scripts will have to be ignored or expensively corrected by editing, looping, or even reshooting. Script clearance is the long-time specialty of de Forest Research Services, founded by a Yale-educated historian, Kellan de Forest, who came west in 1952. "I arrived during the early days of television," says de Forest, who has sold the company but retains an emeritus presence at its headquarters at the corner of Hollywood and Vine. No such service existed before he came along. Research for movies had been a marginal concern of art departments charged with making period pictures look right, though aesthetic decisions often held sway over historical accuracy. To its original client list of motion picture studios, de Forest has added independent film and television production companies, the networks, and advertising agencies, and today some thirty researchers continue to do what the firm has done for four decades, combing scripts for copyright infringement, usage conflict, and all other forms of possible libelousness. One of the company's functions is to ensure that any similarities to actual persons or events in such fictions as *Smoldering Lust* are purely coincidental—or, if the similarities are intended, that they are accurate.

Adding to the day's usual madness at Empire is the constant groaning of the fax machine, depositing page after singlespaced page of de Forest Research Services' script-clearance reports onto a tabletop outside Penny's office. The findings are no-nonsense. For de Forest, it's the details of language and images of *Smoldering Lust* that count, not the arc of the plot line, and certainly not the jokes. To the researchers assigned to the show over the course of the summer—Michelle Teper, Callista Card, Peter Sloman, and Catherine Bennett—the show is purely words on paper, a potentially problematic text (they can enjoy it later). Hence, one of Chris Cody's dyslexic punchlines, "Where'd that chicken's head go?" gets this straight-faced response from de Forest: "No listing among popular American expressions and catch-phrases for one with this exact wording. If you're interested in 'running around like a chicken with its head cut off' or 'Why did the chicken cross the road?' we can help you."

Scrutinizing every line for "E and O"—errors and omissions that could result in legal entanglements—de Forest's reports "are like shark repellent," says Luke Kerner, who now owns the firm. "When it's not safe to go in, we'll tell you how to not get eaten. But it's the producer's call. It happens all the time—people ignore our advice and go swimming in shark-infested waters." Catherine knows that the producers of *Smoldering Lust* may ignore de Forest's cautions. "They're only required to have the research done," she says. "They don't have to heed it."

Part of de Forest's job is to clear proper names for usage, and in its nitty-gritty legal review the firm has made colorful contributions to popular culture. In 1963, Kellan de Forest himself suggested the name Dr. Richard Kimble for *The Fugitive,* after finding real-life counterparts for other names put forth for the TV character. In 1971, he advised Norman Lear to change the name of his new sitcom's lead character Ernest Bunker of Queens, New York, a name de Forest turned up in the Queens phone book. But de Forest is most proud of the name Noah Cross, the evil father and water baron in *Chinatown*. The original name in Robert Towne's screenplay was Joshua Cross, which de Forest found not only in city directories of the period (the thirties) but also in contemporary ones. "The risk of a lawsuit made me uncomfortable," he says, "and I wanted to help find a strong substitute, something also biblical, like Joshua. So I suggested Noah in my report. I gather that Robert Towne and the director, Roman Polanski, liked it very much. With Noah, you have a biblical reference, plus the allusion to water. Penelope Gilliatt singled out the character's name in her review in the *New Yorker*." Nothing so historic happens on the *Smoldering Lust* case, but all character names must be cleared, nonetheless, requiring an extensive name search for each. For Eve Saskatchewan, de Forest finds "no prominent person listed with this exact name in either the U.S. or Canada," concluding "no conflict" on usage. The result is the same for the names of all the other characters except for that of Philip Wingate, which researchers do find in *Who's Who in Science and Engineering*. De Forest urges a change of name to avoid any conflict, but this detail doesn't seem dangerous to the producers; besides, Philip Wingate fits the character so well. But when de Forest urges that the name of Eve's father be changed, the advice sticks. In the show, Eve tells Philip that her father, Richard Garland, is doing some time in a federal prison near Cleveland. But whoa—de Forest has turned up a federal prisoner by that very name, incarcerated in Alabama, and another state prisoner, in Ohio yet, with the same surname.

Brand and corporate names can cause other problems. Though the firm advises deleting the mention of one from the first episode, the scene is filmed as written, with Chris making light of the mess he's made of his white dinner jacket, dubbing it part of Cody Canyon's new "Baskin-Robbins" fashion line. But why would any company object to free publicity? Amazingly, the ice cream company does object, and the line must be changed weeks later in a looping session with John Calvin. Ben and Jerry's obliges the producers' request to use its name, which, luckily enough, has the same number of syllables as that of its uncooperative rival: "Ben and Jerry's" loops perfectly over "Baskin-Robbins."

Unsurprisingly, de Forest finds "no listing for a business in San Francisco or anywhere in the U.S. with [the] exact name" of "Brodsky's Used and Difficult-to-Locate 33 1/3 Record Shop and Detective Agency." The same report also clears usage of "Deep Six Funeral Parlor" in show three.

A background check on the fictional Codys and their business enterprise turns up a number of similarities, including a line of women's clothing manufactured in Vermont, a bar called Cody Creek in North Carolina, and a hobby shop, Cody Creations, in Houston. De Forest notes their existence, though no one could reasonably argue that these actual businesses inspired the creation of the fictional Cody Canyon of *Smoldering Lust*. De Forest also files a lengthy report about a married couple who founded a clothing store and mail-order business. "The estranged couple," states de Forest, "put the company on the auction block" and employees said the husband had affairs with company workers. Shades of Margo, Chris, and Eve! The de Forest search also found two other husband-and-wife entrepreneurial teams who could be construed as counterparts of the Codys.

The reports drone on, but the producers pretty much say to hell with any perceived similarities to actual persons and events. As for the real-life enterprises out there with the name Cody, what better name could there be for western-inspired wilderness chic? But what about those couples who coincidentally could have been models for Margo and Chris? "Husbands and wives start up businesses every day," says Penny. "And sometimes they get divorced because of it. We haven't ripped anybody off." The series is no roman à clef.

Accuracy in storytelling is a welcome incidental benefit that comes with legalistic script review. Backing up series writers with facts, de Forest helps to keep scripts honest. "If Chris Cody walked out of the San Francisco Opera House and jumped onto the BART," says Luke, "we'd point out that that's not possible—there's not a BART station outside the Opera House." Though few viewers would notice the error, Luke doesn't like to let such things pass. "For people in San Francisco, anyway, it could ruin the show, bringing them out of the entertainment," he says. The mistake could also embarrass the producers, the network, and the affiliates: "People love to write letters about little glitches."

CHAPTER TWENTY-TWO
DREAM SEQUENCE

The Pat Williams-Arthur Hamilton theme song, all about infidelity and its consequences, accompanies the show's opening credits, playing behind a titillating montage of grainy black-and-white photographs, the kind a private investigator would submit as evidence that your spouse is indeed fooling around. The first image is of a smartly dressed young woman staring wistfully through parted curtains. Next is a man's hand turning a key to a hotel-room door. There are flowers, a conspicuous bed, two champagne flutes. The camera continues to glide, revealing what the lyrics of the song celebrate: skin touching skin, lips parting. The woman takes the man's necktie, pulls him closer. His bare chest presses against her lacy bustier. Glimpses of inner thigh, ankle, bicep, earlobe. The story ends ambivalently, with the woman back where she was at the beginning, alone at the window, dressed.

Together, song and montage make up what is known as a main-title sequence, a musical and pictorial background of the show's title and top credits. After the words SMOLDERING LUST come the names of the actors: Kate's first, then John's, Alison's, and Bradley's. Next come credits for producers, writers, and directors. Finally, on the last note of music, is the line CREATED BY JAY TARSES. Appearing and dissolving on musical cue, the credits are set in a sleek deco-style typeface that enhances the sequence's romantic echo of another era. Though not as explicit as a Calvin Klein underwear ad, it is risqué for network television—sufficiently so, its designers hope, to keep viewers tuned for the first act.

Nina Saxon and Deborah Ross, the designers, have a knock-out résumé to fax around town to prospective film and TV clients. Their graphics work for television includes *Tat-tinger's, Wings,* and *Sisters*; for film, *The Hand That Rocks the Cradle, My Cousin Vinny, Beauty and the Beast,* and *The Little Mermaid.* At $30,000, the main-title budget for *Smoldering Lust* is about $10,000 less than the figure they'd like, but as Nina says, "This isn't typical network fare, and if we have to pinch and pull a bit and make sacrifices, it's worth it."

Nina and Deborah start work by reading "The Girl in 1216" and playing a cassette tape of Pat Williams's music over and over. "What you pray for," says Deborah at the beginning of the project, "is a good script and a really good song. With Pat and Jay, we're already halfway there." Jay put forth an idea about the main-title sequence in the first draft of show one, calling for "something along the lines of sensuous romantic love paintings of all time, nude and clothed," and he extrapolates on the idea, in a midsummer meeting with Nina and Deborah, asking about "a pictorial history of sex." A kind of album of erotica through the ages in painting, sculpture, photographs, etchings—illustrations from the *Kama Sutra,* a Victorian glimpse of leg, Matisse nudes, a still from the beach scene in *From Here to Eternity,* Fragonard's unblushing lovers in the Codys' bedroom tapestry, revelers chasing nymphs or one another around a Greek urn.

"That's a lot to do in one minute," says Nina. "Centuries of images—Western, Eastern, old, new—won't fit into a smooth sixty-second sequence. The seams will show." She also adds a discouraging note about the cost; getting archival material is increasingly pricey these days. "Reproduction rights to artworks aren't a bargain anymore. Fees have gotten so high, in fact, that it's often less expensive to go out and shoot what you need. So using old pictures doesn't even mean you'll save the client money." Both women are also concerned that the survey could wind up looking too historical, bogging the show down in the past. Certainly such an approach can work, as the view of nineteenth-century Boston does at the beginning of *Cheers*, but the designers are convinced that it's not right for *Smoldering Lust,* which already flirts with the past in its homage to film noir and vintage jazz. They have a better idea, which Nina sums up as a "fantasy tryst." The women make their presentation:

"A man and a woman meet in a hotel room. A charming, romantic hotel."

"It's daytime, maybe lunch hour, her lunch hour. Maybe the man is her boss."

"But there's a dreamy cast to it, like maybe it's not really happening. It could be all in her head. Or his."

"We begin with a shot of her, so maybe what follows is in her imagination."

"She's in a room. The door opens."

"He's brought flowers. They sit on the bed … "

Jay likes what he's heard so far but wants to make sure it's done in the right key, "sensual, not sexy." "Definitely," says Nina. "Nicely turned out people, an elegant setting, just hints of physical contact." Deborah is reassuring: "Bogart and Bacall."

The idea of shooting the sequence as live action is only fleetingly considered. "Too explicit," says Nina. "One wrong move and you cross the line into the Playboy channel." Go with black-and-white photography, Nina suggests, "but in the style of Man Ray. Shadowy and dark, with splashes of color painted on. We'll highlight lips and flowers and fingernails with bits of red and pink and blue and green." After all agree on what the sequence should be, the women go to work.

The first thing to do is write the scenario. Though it contains no dialogue and barely fills a single page, the title-sequence script describes the mood and the movement in such detail that, as Deborah points out, "it tells its own…with … and an end." Think of the minute-long intro as a super-short silent movie and you see why they hired actors rather than models to play the parts. One day's shooting is all they can afford, so no time can be wasted directing the episode. "Models would look right," says Nina, "but we'll be better off with actors who know how to use their bodies to convey emotion. We can't be jumping in asking for more sultriness or anxiety or whatever. With actors, we don't have to take any chances."

A call goes out through casting director Kerry Barden and the auditions he arranges are, according to Nina, "gruesome and hilarious." Gruesome because the scenario brings out "a whole range of painful feelings" from the nearly sixty people who try out over four days, acting out the scene with "real anger, tears, anxiety, and shyness"; hilarious because the auditions are held on the sunny balcony of a photographer's studio in Santa Monica. In full view of passersby, the actors go through the smoldering, lustful motions.

It is clear that there's no wrong way to play the scene, but one couple, Marcy Kaplan and Bruce Savin, stand out. To Marcy the auditions were "like sexual improvisations. We were told to interact with the other person as if we wanted to sleep with each other more than anything in the world—but that, for some reason, we couldn't. It was a difficult scene, and they were smart to hire actors—I'm not sure a model could do that. I'm an actress." It helps, though, that Marcy and Bruce look smashing together: he the tall-dark-handsome type; she, as Dave Brodsky refers to Margo, "fine-looking."

The sequence is shot on location at the Chateau Marmont, not only for its cozy small-hotel looks, appropriate to a make-believe rendezvous, but because the place is accustomed to film and television crews. An industry favorite, the hotel management provides what's necessary (a chic room), charges reasonably for it, then stays out of the way. Working with set dresser Sandra Jordan, Nina and Deborah rearrange the room and dress it, hanging gauzy curtains over the windows and making the bed with Pratesi linens. They bring in lamps, fill vases with roses, place throws over chairs. Nina says she feels as though she's back in film school, scraping by with nickels and dimes. Stopping at a grocery store, she buys fruit, cookies, juice, and bottled water for the actors and crew. "Who can afford a caterer?"

Because the models—rather, actors—do not appear in the actual television series, the camera can only glance at them, so that viewers don't confuse Marcy and Bruce with characters in *Smoldering Lust*. Yet Nina and Deborah must also get close enough to the hotel-room action to convey the heat of the moment, to tell the whispered story of the assignation. "We have to figure out a way to shoot *around* the actors," says Nina. "In order for our story to work, we need to see what they are thinking and feeling." Shooting in profile and in shadow solves part of the problem. So do medium-distance shots. So do extreme close-ups of Marcy and David, which "obscure them a little," says Deborah. "We hope to make them seem like any couple—Everycouple." Still, it does seem likely that viewers will mistake the two in the show's opener for characters in the series. "What can we do?" says Deborah. "If we avoid the actors' faces we'll be left with body parts. And however beautiful those may be, they don't tell the interesting story. You need eyes and mouths for that."

From a total of a hundred or so shots, twenty-six different poses are selected for the sequence. "Thinking like a movie camera," as Nina puts it, she works at an animation board to bring the still images to fluid life, timing the movement to Pat's music.

After adding splashes of color to the pictures and superimposing the credits (in burgundy and tan), the designers deliver the completed job to Empire, on time and on budget. Everyone agrees that it's a pretty piece of work, but is the sequence too pretty, a little too like a fashion spread? Then the inevitable question: Who are these two people, anyway—the Codys? And where are they supposed to be—Room 1216? Many agree with Bradley, who complains that the sequence misrepresents the show in another way. "It makes *Smoldering Lust* look like it's going to be a lot racier than it is," he says. "We don't deliver that much sex."

CHAPTER TWENTY-THREE
ALL WRAPPED UP
AND NOWHERE TO GO

The series wraps on Friday night, September 25. Though not the concluding one of the series, the final scene shot is from the last episode, number thirteen, and introduces another twist in the story line, the coupling of Chris and Cookie in front of a cozy fire in the Cody cabin. Crosscutting with scenes of Margo and Brodsky, who've dropped to another floor, that of the Cody Canyon photography studio, the episode pretty much ends the series where it began, with illicit lust smoldering between principals who have changed partners to try yet another mating dance.

Wrap day is without fanfare. Kate, Bradley, Alison, and Patrick have already completed their work on the show and don't return to celebrate or mourn the final shot. "It would make me too sad," says Kate. At the end of the day, Jay does have a nice surprise in store from cast and crew: a Royal typewriter, circa 1940, of a kind that would be at home on Brodsky's desk. Ruth Bracken, who found the typewriter in a thrift shop near Hancock Park, slips onto the set while Jay is getting coffee. Rolling a blank sheet of paper into the typewriter, she quickly knocks out a single line: 'SMOLDERING LUST—Episode No. 14.' Touched by the gift, Jay thanks the gang and then quickly gets back to work.

Crew members are busy, and not just on wrapping the series and striking the set. For a couple of weeks they've been looking for their next jobs, faxing résumés around town. The crew and production staff would like to move on, but as anxious as nearly everyone is about finding new work, no one wants to commit to a new show if it interferes with returning to this one. Ruth has tentatively lined up a low-budget horror film and a commercial or two. "I need the work," she says, "but it's tricky. If I go with something with a long-term production schedule and *Smoldering Lust* suddenly gets picked up, then that'll leave me out. It's a gamble, and freelancers like me take all the risk. But do I not look for work, taking a chance that NBC will order more episodes? No way! I've got a kid at home. The best I can do is take some short-term jobs and hope I can be done with them if and when we reconvene here."

Until Russ Woody knows what's in store for the show, his writing life is on hold; his dedication to *Smoldering Lust* frustrates his agent, Beth Uffner. HBO is interested in his own series idea, ABC has asked him to write another, but he won't plunge into anything new, not as long as there's a chance to return to the fold. "It's dead, Russ," says Beth, who speaks bluntly to her clients. "Don't waste your time thinking anything good is going to happen between you guys and NBC." Russ, however, who is living proof that some extraordinarily decent people are in demand in Burbank, is not distracted from his heart's goal. "I don't mind working on other things," he says, "as long as it's understood that I can drop them if NBC decides to pick us up." There's been virtually no word from NBC about the fate of *Smoldering Lust,* no hint of an air date, no praise, no pats on the back. The good news, the joke around the set goes, is that Jay got his wish for autonomy, but that's also the bad news. John Calvin, in the potentially career-making role of Chris Cody, is as antsy as anyone and can't resist asking Jay, in a moment between takes of his last scene, what gives with NBC. Jay looks almost sheepish: what's happening or not has become a source of humiliation. "I don't know, John," he says. "It would be nice if someone at the network called and said they've actually had a spare twenty-two minutes to watch one episode and want us to know what a great job we've done, that they like the show and love us all. Yes, that would be nice."

The only word from the network is a rumor: Warren Littlefield, finally having watched a few episodes together, had this to say to Bernie Brillstein: "The show is great, but we don't know what to do with it." And that Bernie blew up: "Goddamn it, Warren, give these people a break! You're killing them. They worked hard for you. It's a good show. Put the fucker on. Put it on in February, March, April, May, I don't care—just give them an air date! You could do an evening of new shows—*Homicide, Smoldering Lust,* whatever else you've got. You have nothing to lose. This show cannot hurt you, it can help you. What's the worse that can happen? The show is paid for, you've already spent the money. No one's going to knock you for making this show. I mean, it's not *Blossom.*"

John is not the only actor to feel the frustration of having his good work sitting around on a shelf, unseen by millions. When Kate complains to Jay, he tells her there's a simple solution to the problem, urging her again to "tell Steven to buy the network. Have your husband buy NBC, then give us Thursday night at 9:30."

Bradley's jest is to enlist the help of Jay's network-honcho daughter. "Can't you get Jamie to slip us onto the schedule? Surely your own daughter can do this one little favor for you. After all, you're the man who put her through college."

"Hell, I got her the job." Jay then seems to turn serious, lashing out less amusingly about "the nitwits who lost *Cheers* and *David Letterman.* Warren's going to be fired. The network's going to go on the block, if it's not already. Paramount's going to buy it, or Barry Diller, someone like that. The whole bunch is going to be fired. What are they doing there, anyway? What shows do they pay attention to if not ours? *Mad About You?* Paul Reiser is shit. I saw the pilot, a rough cut my daughter sent me, and it's horrible. My wife fell asleep and I didn't laugh once. All the development people will be thrown out. My daughter will be fired."

The writers wonder: It wasn't always like this, was it? Wasn't it different back in April, when they got going? Rick Dresser sounds nostalgic about the bright spring day when "Warren called us in to say 'You guys are great. *You're* great, *this* is great.' " But that memory has been pretty well squashed by a newer one, a midsummer script meeting with Kevin Reilly that he still finds baffling. "After scrambling to justify the most general kind of criticisms they finally said, 'Look, we know what we're saying doesn't make sense but believe us on this, bear with us.' What can you say to that? We just stared blankly. I couldn't even write scenes like the ones I've experienced in network meetings—it wouldn't sound credible. Normal people don't say or do things like that in reality. But these are people who can't write, can't direct, can't produce, and can't act, but that's what they want to be part of—it's what they're dealing with every day. There's not really a place for them in the creative process. They just give notes to writers and directors and producers and actors. Mostly the notes are incomprehensible, and when you get a good one and you act on it, you never hear the end of it. It's very 'see-I-told-you-so.' "

Nostalgia creeps into Kevin Reilly's recollections of the early days of *Smoldering Lust,* too. But not for long. "We were in synch at the very beginning," he says. "We were having a good time, and the writers had every reason to like me, since I was advocating the show, getting the company to put money behind it at a time when we were in trouble in the ratings. Not only that, but I was doing it for a writer-producer whose shows were not successes. I fought for *Smoldering Lust* knowing it would get beat up in the ratings. I believed in it at the start and that's what you do for shows you believe in, high-quality shows that get you out of bed in the morning, that make it worthwhile. You fight for them.

"But as I began to see that the show was on the wrong track, heading nowhere, my suggestions to save it were taken as insults. As long as I said nice things about the work, my notes were welcome. But suggest something Jay doesn't like—such as, 'Can we solve this murder anytime soon?' or 'Isn't Chris Cody a little weak?'—and I'm a know-nothing executive."

All summer long, while lust was smoldering between the Codys at Empire Studios, the bad feelings continued to simmer between the network and the show's makers.

"Jay does not have a lot of fans in the upper echelons of the network," says Kevin, making clear that this is a financial, not an aesthetic, judgment. "The perception around here is that there are some writers who mean a lot of money spent and zero returns. Jay's shows don't even export well to other countries. The humor's too narrow—too many in-jokes, too many very specific cultural references. Not even the British would get *Smoldering Lust*."

At a time when networks are conceding small but damaging defeats to cable programmers and are talking about "narrowcasting" to smaller audiences rather than broadcasting to general ones, no one at NBC suggests that *Smoldering Lust* might find a profitable niche. Viewed as an advertising vehicle, the show is akin to an upscale magazine reaching a select audience of the well-to-do who buy expensive cars, who travel, who own second homes. Even so, the network is not likely to indulge any show that scores less than an eight-point overnight rating. (One rating point represents 940,000 viewers.) Routinely, television programmers throw away nine million potential customers, if a viewing audience may be seen as such. "Do you realize," Jay likes to ask, "that the lowest-rated TV show, the bottom of the heap, is seen by more people in one night than all the people who have seen *Hamlet* since it was written?" An overstatement surely, but the whimsical overstatement steels Jay for the expectations and challenges to come, as described by Tony Carey at Brillstein-Grey:

"If we're given a crappy time slot, then we can have some low numbers for a while. No one's going to expect too much. But if we're coming on after *Seinfeld* we better not have even semi-low ratings. Whatever show we're following, we need a higher number than it got. Not necessarily out of the ballpark, but higher than the lead-in. Or we're history, fast."

On December 11 Leslie Dennis delivers the final batch of episodes to the network: shows ten through thirteen, edited, scored, color-corrected, and sound mixed. As the show's film editor, she is responsible for all the details of post-production, the period that describes all the processes that happen after the exposed film leaves Empire. A self-taught craftsman, Leslie describes herself as a daughter-apprentice: Beatrice Dennis was the first woman president of the film editor's union, IATSE. Post-production, says Leslie, "is the stage when you get everything to look and sound right. You pick the best shots, drive the action along by choosing the camera cuts. This is where the electronic wizardry comes in." She works at home using the current Lexus of editing vehicles, the Ediflex, equipped with a bank of twelve television monitors and the kind of computer circuitry that looks as if it could control traffic at a big-city airport. Leslie says it's as simple to operate as it looks; she glides a pencil-sized scanner over the monitors, combining the fragments of film footage into a real piece of storytelling. "It's easy because this machine makes it so simple—I could be sitting here like my mother," says Leslie, visualizing ribbons of film draped around her neck, squinting into a viewfinder, snipping and splicing together all the fragments of celluloid. The work also comes easy because she is used to collaborating with Jay, having edited *Molly Dodd* and then *Slap Maxwell*. Often he is by her side, nodding along with her quick decisions. "At this point I know his rhythms," says Leslie. "He and I don't even have to speak." When she tells him she's completed show thirteen and that the final batch is ready for delivery to the network, he is pleased—as always, she's right on schedule—though not as happy as he might be. Again, the touchy question of an air date, which the network continues to deny the show, remains unanswered.

"They didn't even invite me to that goddamn press dinner," says Jay, referring to NBC's exclusion of *Smoldering Lust* from the Winter Press Tour. It's now the second week of January and over at the Loews Hotel in Santa Monica, limousines are slowly rolling up the circular driveway to drop off those who *have* been invited to the goings-on inside: Mary Tyler Moore, Jerry Seinfeld, Paul Reiser, Phylicia Rashad, Swoosie Kurtz, Lucie Arnaz, Elizabeth Montgomery, Ned Beatty, Jay Leno. They've all come to hype their series, movies, specials, news programs, or late-night entertainments to members of the press, who are gathered here from all across the country, from, as one network enthusiast proclaims, the *Bangor Express* to the *San Diego Union.* The tour does not extend beyond the hotel's seminar rooms, restaurants, and ballroom. Held captive but made extremely comfortable for two weeks, the reporters and critics endure a barrage of publicity and promotion from the four networks and the major cable programmers (Lifetime, MTV, Turner, Nickelodeon): morning, noon, and night, there are screenings of new series, elbow-rubbing parties with stars, interviews with writers and directors, panel discussions with programming executives.

For those who have labored on *Smoldering Lust*, the most disheartening thing about not being asked to participate is that the principals are all available—Jay, Kate, Bradley, John, Alison— and they're chomping to talk about the show. Now is the time to put them on parade, for soon they will disperse—Jay to the East Coast, Bradley to shoot *Philadelphia,* Alison to film *Wyatt Earp,* Kate to join her husband, who is preparing *Schindler's List* in Poland. Effectively releasing the star from from publicity duties, the network draws more ire from Bernie Brillstein. "Are they crazy? They're throwing away Kate's famous name and also her good will. She'll do anything to promote this show. She'll do the press tour. She'll even do *Arsenio*. And what do they do? They say, 'Oh, we won't be needing you. If we do, we can talk to you via satellite.' " It is surprising that Kate's name—or, frankly, her marriage—does not light a fire at the network. But in fact her status—marital, financial—may even be working against her. ("I've heard that Kate's upset," says one NBC hand. "Thinks we haven't paid enough attention to her. Well, while she was working on *Smoldering Lust* we happened to be writing a twenty-two-million-dollar check to her husband for *SeaQuest*.")

Noting that the producers of the *Route 66* remake are on the press tour agenda, Kate is baffled. "They're not even in production yet," she says. Ah, but the network has given that show an air date, which reporters require in order to schedule stories. Without an air date, *Smoldering Lust* may as well not exist—it has such priority with the promotion and publicity people at the network. "We don't go into action until a show is scheduled," says Bob Meyers, the publicist assigned to the show. "Reporters won't even talk to you if you can't say when a show will be broadcast. They have too much else to do with shows that are slotted."

The truth at this moment is that the only Jay NBC is concerned about right now is Jay Leno. The *Tonight Show* debacle dominates the press tour like a wart on NBC's nose. It can't be ignored, no matter what the network would rather talk about or however hard the corporation men try to distract reporters with other news. Inevitably, all questions return to Leno and Letterman. That, and another piece of rotten news for the network: the sudden decision by the creators of *Cheers* to call it quits, leaving NBC with a big empty hole to fill on Thursday nights. Speaking from the ballroom podium, Warren Littlefield tries to steer the topic toward the new shows: "I know all of you have heard previously ... we've announced the series commitment to Steven Spielberg for *SeaQuest* that stars Roy Scheider. In addition, we also have announced Henry Winkler starring in a half-hour comedy for us...

"Steven Bochco and Bill Finkelstein will return to *L.A. Law* as executive producers. They will take over the last eight shows for this season, and they will continue next year as executive producers...

"We're also pleased to say that we now have a deal with George Wendt to star in his next comedy... [And we have] purchased the novel *Den of Lions,* which will be released in October... This will be a four-hour miniseries about the plight of Terry Anderson as a hostage in Lebanon...

"There will be, in the next few weeks, another wave of program announcements for the fall. I have a number of exciting things that we're currently in negotiation on."

He talks about moving *Seinfeld* to a new time slot, of scooping CBS on Lucie Arnaz's stash of Lucy and Desi home movies, and plans to premiere Barry Levinson's *Homicide* on Super Bowl Sunday. The announcements, however, are pretty much lost in recurring questions about Leno's future at the network—and Warren's too. "Did you ever consider firing Leno?" someone in the audience asks. "Do *you* worry about being fired?"

The interrogation doesn't end with Leno's arrival in the ballroom—on his Harley. A raucous entrance, but the beleaguered talk-show host handles the questions gracefully and, it seems, honestly, describing how it's felt all these months to dangle at the end of the network rope. He cracks jokes, of course, telling the audience he now knows what NBC stands for: Never Believe Contracts. He ends the routine by telling (not asking) Warren to wheel the big bike off the stage. A good sport, Warren plays parking valet then returns to the stage to adjourn the session and announce that he and his colleagues will linger on for any further questions.

Smoldering Lust has been mentioned in *TV Guide* and *Entertainment Weekly,* so there is inevitable curiosity about its absence from the schedules. Warren's answer—"*Smoldering Lust?* We'll probably put it on mid-season … Could catch on"—is as rushed and vague as those of his fellows. Perry Simon, of primetime development: "Oh, it's so special … the kind we have to put in the right slot. It's like *Northern Exposure*—it needs special attention." Kevin Reilly: "Brilliant … We're working on getting the right time slot for it. It could catch on."

All around the hotel lobby, in big kiosks crowned with cardboard NBC peacocks, the day's activities are spelled out in cutout construction-paper letters, the kind school children pin to classroom bulletin boards. Press kits—fat three-ring binders crammed with new-program lineups, star bios, and exclamatory press releases— have been produced for reporters whose credentials, worn around the neck, are stamped with their affiliation: the *Kansas City Star,* the *Des Moines Register,* the *Edmonton Journal,* the *Memphis Commercial Appeal,* the *Austin American-Statesman,* the *Los Angeles Times.* A suite has been set aside for their use, done up like a newsroom with telephones and fax machines and IBM Selectrics. But the room is quiet most of the time; this event, after all, doesn't necessitate earth-shaking dispatches.

Except for that moment in the ballroom when the programming and development executives are put on the spot about the new show by Jay Tarses, nothing is uttered about "Smoldering *what?*" (as one reporter reacts to the title). In the hotel's ocean-front restaurant, the NBC publicist Rosemary O'Brien admits that she hasn't even seen the show, though all thirteen episodes have been delivered to the network. "I loved *Molly Dodd,* though," she says. "Is it anything like that?" One of those she's treating to lunch, Alan Carter from *Entertainment Weekly,* can't answer the question because he hasn't seen the show either, and asks her when screening copies will be made available to the media. "You know the answer to that, Alan," says Rosemary. "Whenever we get an air date."

Throughout the two-day fest, NBC keeps *Smoldering Lust* out of the picture, and virtually all the reporters and critics leave Santa Monica knowing nothing of the show's existence, unaware that they were denied the opportunity to talk one-to-one with the cast and creator. One, Matt Roush of *USA Today*, wages a guess about the exclusion. "They resent the show, which is an unwanted inheritance from the Tartikoff era. The new regime must feel saddled by it. They'll air it, all right, but not with any enthusiasm. Only out of deference to Tarses and Tartikoff. Rather than *Smoldering Lust* they should call it *Lingering Respect*." Poor Jay.

"Not 'poor Jay,'" says Roush. "It's too bad the show's not going to be a player, this or any other season. But it's hard to feel sorry for someone like Jay Tarses. Yes, he's failed. But he's one of the richest failures in Burbank."

CHAPTER TWENTY-FOUR
"GOOD MORNING," HE LIED

Through the winter and well into spring, it is depressingly obvious that *Smoldering Lust* is not going to appear on NBC's schedule anytime soon, not even as a "midseason replacement," when it might have gotten a crack at survival by taking over a niche where another has died out. Finally, on April 22, 1993, seven months after the final scene was shot, NBC breaks its silence about the show with news of an air date. No press conference is called, and no enthusiasm greets the announcement—not in the network's solemn halls, not on entertainment pages around the country. There's a dismissive, leftover quality to the news when it appears in the trade papers, and the details are discouraging: the network has slotted the show for Saturday nights at ten (between *Mad About You* and *The Powers that Be)*. The premiere won't be just any Saturday night, but May 29, during Memorial Day weekend.

"How many people will be home watching that night?" Jay says. "Twelve?" The one promising aspect of the plan is a one-hour format: the first two episodes will run back to back, creating an "event" that will, it is hoped, give viewers a doubly enticing dose of *Smoldering Lust.*

Defenders of the summer launch—all network employees, not surprisingly—include Kevin Reilly, who cites the June debut of *Northern Exposure,* a surprise ratings success. "Little jewels like that can get lost in the crowd of a new fall schedule. Summer doldrums can be good for their long-term survival." Bernie Brillstein slaps down that argument. "Don't believe that summer season crap for a second. Sure, a few shows may come off the summer, but always by accident. It's a dumping ground. It would serve them right if some really high numbers start coming in and NBC has to pay huge fees to extend the options for Kate and everyone else." He is referring to a clause in the actors' contracts that keeps them beholden to the series until June 15. The Memorial Day debut cuts it close, allowing only three airings before the network must decide if it will renew. Alison Elliott, considering a number of other movie offers, asks Nevin Dolcefino at Innovative Artists what to expect. It's a question without an answer right now. "It's anyone's guess," says Nevin, who counsels his client not to be discouraged by the air date. "They're getting it on before June 15, which gives the network time to measure the audience reaction. If they were going to kill the series, they'd put it on after the options have expired, otherwise they'd pay dearly to renegotiate. I don't think they've written the show off. But let's wait and see."

Not two weeks later, a bombshell falls: NBC is changing the title of the show back to Brandon Tartikoff's original idea, *Black-Tie Affair*. The reason cited: *Smoldering Lust* is confusing. "Surveys show that viewers don't understand the title," says Patricia Schultz, the head of network press relations. When Jay learns of the change, he is indignant, telling reporters that "NBC has not only violated my creative rights, but has driven a stake into the heart of this show. The new title has nothing to do with the series and does not even evoke its comedic nature." The stories, the characters, the situations, he says, "won't make sense under the new title," and he's quite right. When Brodsky rambles on at the top and bottom of every episode about so-and-so's "smoldering lust," viewers will miss the spirit in which the words are written and spoken. "The humor is poisoned," says Jay, swearing that he'll never work for NBC again, calling its treatment of him "the worst of my career." Executives there, he announces, "are liars, the enemy of talent."

By the time Warren gets around to calling him about the new title, Jay is ready. "I'm sure you didn't know about this before now," he says. "You just run the place, that's all." Defending the decision as simply a matter of good marketing, Warren asks if Jay has a better idea for a new title—something zippier than *Black-Tie Affair* but not as obscure as *Smoldering Lust*. Yes, as a matter of fact, he does. "How about *Dicks and Cunts*?" he says, then slams down the telephone.

TV *Guide* chides NBC for the title change, and its advance review of the show is lukewarm, comparing it unfavorably to *Molly Dodd* and *Buffalo Bill*. *Entertainment Weekly's* grade of C-minus is another blow, coming from a magazine whose readers might have given the show a shot. "In this tired half-hour comedy," writes the *EW* critic, "there's a murder you won't care about, a couple of cartoon smooches between Capshaw and Whitford, and a recital of manufactured drolleries that stand in for wit." Howard Rosenberg of the *Los Angeles Times* is also turned off, stating that "the gap separating Tarses from the rest of humankind" has widened with *Black-Tie Affair,* the humor of which he compares to "one of those high-pitched whistles that only dogs hear."

Others around the country do like the show. *The Chicago Sun-Times* praises the "hot, sophisticated humor for discerning adults who shun simple-minded sitcoms" while hinting that viewers should "enjoy it while it lasts." *The Philadelphia Inquirer* urges a write-in campaign, "to confound the brain trust at NBC ... Watch the show [and] force the network to order more episodes, just as you forced CBS to continue with another summer series, 'Northern Exposure.' " *People* calls the series "a refreshing baker's dozen ... "

Jay's well reported war with NBC undermines the tame publicity materials disseminated by the network, a standard-issue press kit containing that smashing cast photograph. Combined with the dim spot on the prime-time schedule, the tepid campaign seems less like a push for a new show than a disgruntled goodbye to damaged goods. It is rumored that Kate, who has been receiving the bad news via faxes to Poland, fires off one to Warren, sarcastically thanking him for making her first television experience a nightmare.

When May 29 rolls around, the main-title sequence for *Black-Tie Affair* plays without the *Smoldering Lust* lyrics, just Pat William's music over the montage. Arthur Hamilton, his words to the song on the cutting room floor, feels sad for Sue Raney. "I had a feeling that the song might've had a life on the radio." For Sue, it's a lost opportunity to be heard by a huge audience. "I'm crushed," she says. "Not that I thought that this would be my big break—my name flies by so fast in tiny type in the end credits you can't even read it. But it would have been nice, that's all. You never know, the song might have gone somewhere."

For a holiday weekend, the first episode pulls a decent number in the overnight Nielsen rating, a 6.6—about six million viewers. But the ratings picture is a large one, and each show is graded against its predecessor in the schedule. And NBC's audience report for the evening of May 29 reflects doubly bad news for *Black-Tie Affair.* The lead-in, a rerun of *Mad About You,* pulls an 8.2, meaning that *Black-Tie Affair's* score represents a dropoff in viewers. The figure for episode two, piggybacked onto the first for the special one-hour premiere, dropped a few points lower. The news gets worse for the series as it plays out the summer run, June 5, 12, and 19, bringing small but telling declines in the ratings.

On Monday, June 28, NBC abruptly cancels the show. The news is like a frying pan slammed over the head. Yes, the numbers weren't great, but they weren't in the cellar either, especially for Saturday nights in summer. And besides, the thirteen episodes are completed, and production is shut down: what harm is there in airing them? No replacement series will generate any higher advertising revenues for summer prime-time spots that were pre-sold in January. "We had to cut our losses" is all Preston Beckman will say. What losses? The show's expenses already have been met, the commercials set for Ben-Gay, Downy, L'Oreal, Planter's Peanuts. Certainly the decision to pull the plug demonstrates to advertisers that the network is decisive; it will not tolerate poor performers that loll around in the lower Nielsens. Specifically, it won't indulge programs that appeal to older viewers, as this particular comedy may be guilty of. For a year now, NBC has tried to hold fast to its decision to court what in Burbank are defined as younger viewers (those who fall between the ages of eighteen to forty-nine). That strategy led to the deliberate and controversial cancellation of at least one hit show, *The Golden Girls,* as if its fans were stingy senior citizens whose spending days were over. "Find the logic in that!" Bernie Brillstein says. "You kill a hit show because its viewers don't necessarily watch MTV or *The Simpsons?* Because the audience may be in their fifties and sixties? Who do they think has more money? They're talking about me. They'd dump me. I'm sixty-two and I buy a lot more stuff than my grown children do. I'm a lot richer than my kids."

In the summer of 1993, when NBC's press, advertiser, and affiliate relations are near disastrous—there is the loss of *Cheers,* the Leno-Letterman debacle, and the false-reporting charges admitted to by *Prime Time Live*—perhaps the network needs to show the industry that it will not tolerate an ill-tempered ranks-breaker like Jay Tarses. The cancellation of his show does seem punitive, like the playing out of personal grudge against the fallen man who for weeks has hurled very public insults at NBC. This individual-versus-corporation battle ends the way Paddy Chayefsky in *Network* said all such confrontations would: the broadcast giant wins, and wins crushingly.

After Jay's tantrums, it is of course impossible to find an executive at NBC who sounds sad about the end of *Smoldering Lust* or contrite about its dismissal. Even Brandon Tartikoff, though he compliments Jay on "taking my original idea so far," finds the tone of the work "way off, and in no way commercial." The series wasn't around long enough to woo the kind of dedicated audiences that organized protests and won temporary respite for such shows as *I'll Fly Away* and *Brooklyn Bridge* and the result of its failure, Brandon fears, is that Jay and writers like him will be relegated to a "boutique league" or branded as a kind of "off-Broadway" of Burbank. That, he says, would be a shame, "because the truth is that Jay really is Neil Simon—his comedy is that strong. He just chooses not to pull the trigger."

"It's too bad that Jay's decided to work in network television," says Kevin Reilly, suggesting that the writer belongs in another, less commercial medium, probably cable. Apparently the New York theater is not Jay's for the taking, not if the reaction to the Playwrights Horizons staging of *Man in His Underwear* (produced earlier in Williamstown, Massachusetts) is a fair indicator. Though the play was not open to the press, word of mouth was not encouraging about this evening spent with an irascible protagonist, an older Chris Cody and somewhat more successful in flirting with marital infidelity. Trudging along from jokes about lingerie to ones about condoms, *Man in His Underwear* takes a dated look at the battle of the sexes, playing like an extended Playboy party joke.

Though the ashes of *Smoldering Lusts* are cold now, the experience always will be galling to its creator. "How old do we have to be before we realize they're all a bunch of lying scumbags?" Jay asks, recalling the fleeting bit of rah-rah the network faked for the series. "Hey, we spent nine million bucks on the show, so whether we like it or not we're going to get behind it." Who at the network said that? Kevin, Warren—or perhaps Don Ohlmeyer, the veteran of sports telecasting recently brought in over Warren in a dramatic corporate shuffle? NBC seems content with the prospect of not ever again working with the "maverick rebel on the periphery," as Jay characterized himself during the stormy few weeks that *Smoldering Lust*—rather, *Black-Tie Affair*—was on the air. "I'm just a hired gun," he said, indicating that if he returned to television it will have to be on his rootin'-tootin' creative terms. No one, for instance, had better try to force a laugh track on him. "There will never be a laugh track, as long as I'm alive." For now, he suggests, not at all seriously, he will begin his first novel. A showbiz novel set in Burbank. He's already got the first line: " 'Good morning,' he lied."

My adventure in Burbank at an end, I've wondered: Might the series have succeeded if all thirteen episodes had aired, in a hot spot on a good night, and under the original title? No way. Score another victory for the philistines, the producers might say, but it is hard to imagine even the most fervent admirers of *Molly Dodd* and *Buffalo Bill* tuning in to *Black-Tie Affair* week after week. Though Jay betters sitcom caricatures by creating a gallery of recognizable human beings—Margo, Chris, Eve, Brodsky, Cookie—this time his characters are bogged down in a nearly plotless story.

People look blank when asked if they ever heard of or saw *Black-Tie Affair,* but the widespread ignorance about the show really does no damage to anyone associated with it. The powers in Burbank are familiar with the series and acknowledge what was fine about it—the production design, the music, the wardrobe, much of the writing. No casting chiefs will forget who won the starring roles, either. Word is out that John Calvin can indeed handle the lead in a romantic comedy. Kate was a revelation as the pensive Margo, and taking the womanly role was a splendid career move (lacking only the audience). Bradley and Alison may still be looking for the legendary big break offered by network visibility, but their agents at Innovative Artists continue to book them in high-profile films. Meanwhile, thirteen episodes of *Black-Tie Affair* looks just fine on their resumes.

The confused and unhappy business end of the series should make networks and producers study the kind of unrestricted multiple-episode deals this enterprise may have enjoyed during production but eventually came to regret. As the episodes piled up on Warren Littlefield's desk, the writers and actors were left to work in a vacuum, deprived of feedback from colleagues and viewers. Had Jay just once turned an ear toward NBC executives (who have, after all, indulged such slow starters as *St. Elsewhere* and *Cheers),* he might have heard some advice that could have saved his show. More importantly, had NBC aired the first few episodes while the series was still in production, public reaction to the work might have helped the writers and even the actors clarify and liven up the story. Interference from the cretins, Jay might say, but it's the same process that benefits playwrights in the theater, when new work goes into preview performances.

Well, better luck next time. You hear that rather a lot in Burbank, where the next time can come around again with astonishing speed. The business of TV happens quickly, and to a young development executive like Kevin Reilly, that is the thrill of it. "Someone comes in with an idea," he says. "Any idea—about a grandmother and a dog, or a dog's grandmother. And *wham!* You go straight to writing scripts, casting, shooting. All in eight to twelve weeks—boom, boom, boom! It's on the air and millions of people are watching. It's exhilarating, like being on a fast train." The ride has lots of scary turns of course, as Kevin experienced not for the first time with *Smoldering Lust.* It's true that someone probably should have prevented this expensive disaster from happening, but apparently it has left behind no injuries more serious than wounded pride. "Look what gets on the air," says Jay, sounding a decades-old note of disgust about the low quality of programming as he plans his next strikes—a sitcom for Fox (laugh track and all), and maybe a vehicle for Kate, whose knockout work as Margo was a revelation to the few who managed to catch the series' comet-like streak across their television screens. Whether his latest work soars or crashes, Jay is a player for keeps, admired and revered. Producers will line up to hear his next pitch. An actor's dream, a Tarses production will always attract top talent. Something of a Burbank legend now, Jay Tarses informs and influences programming even when he doesn't have a show on air. A year or so after the demise of *Smoldering Lust*, NBC announced the coming of *Madman of the People*, a comedy the network was pushing with muscle it never flexed for Jay's latest late effort. The forthcoming show stars Dabney Coleman as a gruff columnist for a failing magazine who must contend with the hot-shot, kick-butt executive hired to turn things around. The young executive turns out to be — fun surprise — the columnist's bossy daughter. Overseeing the series at NBC is — another fun surprise — Jamie Tarses. On screen and behind the scenes: fathers and daughters in competition and combat. Any similarities between the father and daughter of *Madman* and Jay and Jamie Tarses are anything but coincidental. Even in Burbank, art imitates life.

AFTERWORD
BY KEN LEVINE

TV writers don't get a lot of sympathy when they complain. All jobs come with a certain amount of frustration, but most people would gladly trade with TV writers. Their lives seem so glamourous. Work in a movie studio. Drive Teslas. Get to go to the *People's Choice Awards*. But would you trade careers with a fire fighter? Because that's what a TV writer who is running his own show essentially is.

Even under the best of conditions, when your show is a big hit and the network pretends to trust you, you're still putting out fires. Daily. Don't think you're spending your days lounging in the firehouse reading Variety and washing the truck. You're always on the move with the siren blaring. If you're lucky you get five hours sleep. And again, that's on a hit show where everything is going smoothly. But here's the thing — with a hit show all the fires can be *contained*.

Now imagine a show that's in trouble. Wildfires are burning out of control in seven remote locations and you've only got one truck. All of a sudden that assembly line is looking pretty good to ya.

Smoldering Lust is the perfect title for a book on the evolution of a failed TV series. And make no mistake, for every hit there are fifty misses. There are not enough flame retardant planes to handle them.

My first staff job was on *The Tony Randall Show* for MTM. I was hired by Jay Tarses and his then-partner, Tom Patchett. They had just come off running *The Bob Newhart Show*. I could not have had a better show runner and mentor than Jay Tarses. He and Tom ran that show like a well-oiled machine. And yet, there were actor issues on occasion, network demands, script problems — fires (albeit trash can fires; not all of Malibu).

My point is no one was more talented and better equipped than Jay Tarses to launch a new hit sitcom. Plus, he surrounded himself with the best talent in town. And yet, the Santa Ana winds were blowing. Author Vance Muse does a masterful job of putting you right on the front line.

Now when you read about the casting hassles and the network meddling you might be thinking "Well, yeah, but that's from a bygone era. Today we're in a different world, a streaming world. Would a scenario like this even occur today?"

The answer is yes.

For two reasons.

Just because Netflix and Apple and Hulu aren't NBC or CBS doesn't mean they're giving the creator unlimited creative control. They give notes like anyone else. They may not be as ham-fisted and dogmatic but they make their opinions known.

And second, everyone in the industry has predicted that major broadcast networks are if not dead then at least on hospice. Audience shares dwindle every year. But I think the WGA strike of 2023 prompted TV writers to re-examine the landscape. Many realized that if they brought their show to a streaming service like Netflix that Netflix would own the show outright. You are essentially salaried to produce it. And you'll only get an order of six or maybe ten episodes at a time. Even if your show is a big streaming hit, they'll only need about thirty episodes. After that it gets expensive for them so they'd rather cut bait and look for something else.

But if you brought your show to NBC you could still be a profit participant. If it's a hit you make 22 a year instead of 10 every year-and-a-half. And you could make 100 of them instead of 30. Finally, you could then sell the series to Netflix and get an additional payday.

So creators are returning to the networks. But that means crushing interference and all the roadblocks that Tarses & company put up with on *Black Tie Affair* or whatever it was called at different times.

So the stories from 30 years ago are the same stories today. Sound the fire alarm.

⚜ ⚜ ⚜

Ken Levine is an Emmy winning writer/director/playwright/ major league baseball announcer/cartoonist. Ken was the Head Writer of *MASH*, Producer of *Cheers*, and has written over 200 episodes of television for such shows as *MASH, Cheers, Frasier, The Simpsons,* and *Wings.* He co-wrote the movie *Volunteers* starring Tom Hanks & John Candy, has been the play-by-play voice of the Baltimore Orioles, Seattle Mariners, and San Diego Padres, contributes cartoons to the *New Yorker* magazine, and hosts the podcast *Hollywood and Levine.*

www.ingramcontent.com/pod-product-compliance
Lightning Source LLC
Chambersburg PA
CBHW030824090426
42737CB00009B/869